|| न हि ज्ञानेन सदृशं पवित्रमिह विद्यते ||

Pūrṇa Vidyā

(Vedic Heritage Teaching Programme)

Īśvara and Religious Discipline

Part 7

*"One's wisdom and appreciation of beauty manifests through various forms of one's culture.
And the study of one's cultural heritage leads one to the appreciation of beauty and wisdom in life."*
Swami Dayananda

D1377909

Swamini Pramananda and Sri Dhira Chaitanya

Editor: Irene Schleicher

Copyright 2000
Swamini Pramananda and Sri Dhira Chaitanya
All rights reserved. No part of this publication may be reproduced, stored in a retrival system, or transmitted, in any form or by means - electronic, mechanical, photocopying, recording, or otherwise - without the prior written permission of the authors.

FIRST EDITION 2000
REPRINT 2001
REVISED EDITION 2004
REPRINT 2008
REPRINT 2009
REPRINT 2010
REPRINT 2011
REPRINT 2012

Published by
Swamini Pramananda and Sri Dhira Chaitanya

Books Available at:

In India

Purna Vidya Trust, Headquarters
"Mamatha", # 8A, Basement,
North Gopalapuram IInd Street,
Chennai – 600086 (India)
Phone: 044-2835 2593
E. Mail: **purnavidyachennai@gmail.com**

In U.S.A
E.Mail: **purnavidyausa@gmail.com**
Phone: 1-718-501-4785

In U.K
E.Mail: **purnavidya.uk@gmail.com**
Phone: +44-19522-73543

For more information on other Books/Cds/ Vcds of Purna Vidya visit the website: **http://www.purnavidya.com**

Printed in the USA-Charleston, South Carolina

सरस्वति नमस्तुभ्यं वरदे कामरूपिणी।
विद्यारम्भं करिष्यामि सिद्धिर्भवतु मे सदा।।

sarasvati namastubhyaṃ varade kāmarūpiṇī
vidyārambaṃ kariṣyāmi siddhirbhavatu me sadā

"Salutation to you O Goddess *Sarasvati*, who is a giver of boons, and who has a beautiful form! I begin my studies. Let there be success for me always."

Table of Contents

Message from Swamiji

Dear Children,

Learning is play if you enjoy learning. Here is a book of learning made enjoyable. You learn Vedic Heritage through solving puzzles and playing games testing your memory and rational thinking. By studying this book you will not only learn Vedic Heritage, but also the art of learning. You have my best wishes and love,

Yours,

Sw. Dayananda

A Note to Children

Dear Children,

We welcome you to the challenging games, fun-filled projects that make up the exercises of the text books that you will be studying and we commend you for your commitment to the study of the Vedic Heritage.

In these exercises, situations are presented which test your understanding of the nature of the Lord and forms of worship. The games also include the topic of religious disciplines that you may have seen in your homes and are presented to you in a form that lends itself to easy understanding.

There are sections such as "Points to Ponder", "Answer these questions" and "Journal Writing" which are thought provoking and meant for class discussions. For your own assimilation of certain topics, we have provided sections such as "Practice at home" and "Field Work".

As children we imbibe cultural forms of expression and practices by observing those around us. However we often perform actions without fully understanding their purpose and meaning. This book will help you to discover the deep meanings behind our cultural and traditional practices. You will thereby be able to enjoy the richness of our heritage and carry it with pride and honour.

We hope that as you explore these pages, you will discover the richness of your Vedic culture. We wish you many hours of enjoyment and learning as you study your heritage.

With love and best wishes,

Swamini Pramananda Saraswati
Sri Dhira Chaitanya

Key to Transliteration

Key to Transliteration and Pronunciation of Sanskrit Letters

Since Sanskrit is a highly phonetic language, accuracy in articulation of the letters is important. For those unfamiliar with the *Devanāgarī* script, the international transliteration is a guide to proper pronunciation of Sanskrit letters.

अ *a* (but)
आ *ā* (mom)
इ *i* (it)
ई *ī* (beet)
उ *u* (put)
ऊ *ū* (pool)
ऋ *ṛ* (rhythm)
ए *e* (play)
ऐ *ai* (high)
ओ *o* (toe)
औ *au* (loud)
क *k* (skate) 1
ख *kh* (blockhead)*1
ग *g* (gate) 1
घ *gh* (loghut)*1
ङ *ṅ* (sing) 1
च *c* (chunk) 2
छ *ch* (catch him)*2
ज *j* (john) 2
झ *jh* (hedgehog)*2
ञ *ñ* (bunch) 2
ट *ṭ* (start)*3
ठ *ṭh* (anthill)*3
ड *ḍ* (dart)*3
ढ *ḍh* (godhead)*3
ण *ṇ* (under)*3
त *t* (path)*4
थ *th* (thunder)*4
द *d* (that)*4
ध *dh* (breathe)*4
न *n* (numb)*4
प *p* (spin) 5
फ *ph* (loophole)*5
ब *b* (bin) 5
भ *bh* (abhor)*5
म *m* (much) 5
य *y* (young)
र *r* (drama)
ल *l* (luck)
व *v* (in between wile and vile)
श *ś* (shove)
ष *ṣ* (bushel)
स *s* (so)
ह *h* (hum)
ṃ *anusavāra* (nasalisation of preceding vowel)
ḥ *visarga* (aspiration of preceding vowel)
* No exact English equivalents for these letters
1-guttural; 2-palatal;3-lingual; 4-dental;5-labial

Īśvara and Religious Disciplines

Īśvara and Religious Disciplines

INTRODUCTION TO *ĪŚVARA*

When one looks at oneself, one sees oneself to be an individual living in this world, responding to various objects, situations and people. One also sees an intelligent design throughout the entire creation. There are stars, planets and satellites that function in an orderly manner. The earth moves in its own orbit as even the other planets do. The sun never fails to rise, the oceans never dry up and all the elements function within the framework of physical laws. The various forms of life live in a complex interdependent relationship. A human body, like other life-forms, is made up of many components, each having a distinct function. Every organ and cell in the body seems to have a definite purpose. There is nothing that is redundant in this vast creation. The exquisite order and beauty of the creation indicates the presence of a cause which is intelligent.

Who is *Īśvara*?

The creation of any object, such as a pot, involves a twofold cause. One is the creator, the pot-maker, who has the knowledge and the skill to make the pot. The other is the material from which the pot is made, for example, clay. In Sanskrit, the intelligent cause is called *nimitta-kāraṇa* and the material cause is called *upādāna-kāraṇa*.

The creation, being intelligently put together, must also have an intelligent cause. Just as the creator of an object must have the knowledge of his creation, so too, the creator of the world must have knowledge of his entire creation. Therefore, omniscience, all knowledge, must reside with the creator. The creation must also have a material cause, the material from which it is made. Here the question arises as to whether the material exists apart from the creator. In the case of the clay pot, the material, the clay, exists apart from the pot-maker who uses the clay in order to create the clay pot. In the case of the creation, however, one is unable to assume that the material cause is separate from the intelligent cause. If the intelligent cause were separate from its material cause, the intelligent cause would have to exist outside the creation. Since outside and inside are concepts used in reference to space, and space itself is part of creation, nothing can exist apart from the creation. Therefore, the intelligent cause can only be non-separate from the creation.

Furthermore, if the intelligent cause were separate from the creation, another question would arise as to where the material cause for the creation came from. If one presumed the existence of another material cause for the creation, the question would arise as to the source of that material. This would lead to the fallacy of infinite regression, because the source of the first material cause would rest in another material cause, whose source would rest in another material cause, and so on, leading to an indefiniteness in conclusion.

There is a finality of perception, however, because one does see a creation. Seeing the creation, one must account for its material cause. Therefore, one can only infer that the material cause of the creation cannot be separate from the intelligent cause.

Examples of both the intelligent and material causes resting in one entity are not unknown in one's experience. When one dreams, for example, one creates an entire dream world. The dreamer is the intelligent cause of the dream. The material cause from which the various objects in the dream are made is not separate from the dreamer. It is the thoughts and memories of the dreamer which make up the dream. Another example is a spider who spins a web. The spider has the knowledge of how to make the web and finds the material to do so within himself.

The one who is thus both the intelligent and the material cause for the whole creation is known as *Īśvara*, the Lord.

Īśvara - He or She?

One generally uses the pronoun He for *Īśvara*. This is only a convention and does not imply that *Īśvara* has a gender.

In the creation one sees both the masculine and the feminine genders. A gender indicates functional and anatomical differences between living organisms. Gender differences do not extend beyond these differences. There is no male eye, female hunger, or neuter sadness. Looking at the world comprising all three genders one cannot attribute only one gender to *Īśvara*. One can only say that *Īśvara* is not male, female, or neuter; or one can say that *Īśvara* is male, female and neuter, being the cause of everything.

The intelligent aspect of *Īśvara* is called *puruṣa*, which is masculine and the material aspect is called *prakṛti* or *māyā* which is feminine. This combination of the male and the female aspects in *Īśvara* is represented in the form of the deity called *Ardhanārīśvara*, which is half male and half female.

Where is *Īśvara*?

One does not encounter *Īśvara* as a resident of any particular place. Were he a resident of a particular place in the creation a question would arise as to where he was before the creation of the universe. Let one assume that *Īśvara* is an individual entity living in a particular place that is not available for one's immediate perception, for example, heaven. If this were so, where was he before he created heaven? Saying that he lived in another heaven or hell leads to the same problem of infinite regression.

Looking at the example of the dream, if one were to ask where in the dream world the dreamer is located, one would see that, with respect to the dream world, the dreamer is every where in it. The dream mountains, dream rivers, dream animals and dream people are not separate from the dreamer. The dreamer pervades the dream. In other words, the dreamer is immanent in the dream. Similarly, if *Īśvara* is the intelligent and material cause of the creation, he is immanent in the creation; there is nothing in the creation that is apart from *Īśvara*. This is what is meant when one says that *Īśvara* is all pervasive or omnipresent.

Even though the dreamer pervades the dream, the dreamer is not the dream. It is the dream world that resolves into the dreamer. In other words, the dreamer is the one who pervades the dream and at the same time transcends it. In the same manner, *Īśvara* pervades the creation and transcends it.

Therefore, to find *Īśvara* one does not need to look for a distinct individual being because the creation does not exist apart from *Īśvara*. In fact, the creation is nothing but *Īśvara*.

EXERCISE

I. Discover the truth! Choose the correct answer.

1. The creation
   a) presupposes an intelligent cause
   b) does not require any cause
   c) is born out of the Big Bang

2. The creation requires
   a) heat to create
   b) a material from which it is made
   c) no material at all

3. The spider and its web illustrates
   a) pot as different from clay
   b) the material cause is not separate from the intelligent cause
   c) that the creator lives in heaven

4. *Īśvara*
   a) lives in heaven
   b) is non-separate from the creation
   c) does not exist

5. The form of *Ardhanārīśvara* reveals the Lord as
   a) a male
   b) a female
   c) a combination of male and female

6. The human body is
   a) an intelligent creation
   b) disorderly in nature
   c) a creation which has no purpose

7. The Lord as both intelligent and material cause is illustrated in
   a) the story of Adam and Eve
   b) the pot example
   c) the dream example

II. True or False. *Check one.*

1. All that exists in the creation serves a purpose. [T] [F]

2. Before the creation of heaven *Īśvara* lived in hell. [T] [F]

3. The Lord is masculine in gender. [T] [F]

4. *Īśvara* is present everywhere. [T] [F]

5. The Vedic vision supports the statement that there is no God. [T] [F]

III. Points to Ponder:

1. Share a time with the class when you were out in nature, for example, at the mountains or at the ocean. Did the glories of nature inspire you to appreciate the existence of the Lord?

   ____

   ____

   ____

2. The religious culture of India is based on the fact that the creator is non-separate from the creation. Illustrate three forms of worship which reveal this fact.

   ____

   ____

   ____

ĪŚVARA THE ELEMENTS

In Sanskrit, the creation is known as *viśva* which means "*vividha-pratyaya-gamyam*" - that which consists of many and varied forms. The *Vedas* reduce all of these forms to five constituent elements, called the *pañca-mahābhūtas*, five great elements. They are *ākāśa*, space; *vāyu*, air; *agni*, fire; *āpaḥ*, water; and *pṛthivī*, earth.

In this five-elemental model of the creation, the creation is seen as nothing but these five great elements which have undergone a process of grossification. These elements are thus present in every object in varying degrees. For example, a living object occupies space; is composed of air, water and earth; and contains fire, in the form of temperature. Even inanimate objects, such as water, have the qualities of five great elements. Water occupies space; is composed of air, in the form of hydrogen and oxygen molecules; contains fire, in the form of temperature; and contains earth, in the form of minerals and organic elements.

As the creation is non-separate from *Īśvara*, the five great elements that comprise the creation are worshipped as *Īśvara*. There are five temples in India where *Īśvara* is invoked in each of the five elements. These temples are:

Chidambaram

At the Chidambaram Temple in Tamil Nadu, Lord *Śiva* is worshipped as the element space. The temple contains an altar which has no idol; instead it has a mirror draped with a golden garland of *bilva* leaves to which prayers are offered. After *ārati* is offered to the *śivaliṅga* in the sanctum, it is also offered to the Lord in the form of space. This form of worshipping space is called the *Cidambara-rahasya*, or the secret of Chidambaram. The Chidambaram Temple is also famous for its deity, Lord *Naṭarājā*, the dancing *Śiva*.

Kalahasti

In the main sanctum of the *Śiva* temple in Kalahasti, Andhra Pradesh, is a *śivaliṅga*, as well as a lamp with a constant flame. The temple has been designed so that a slight draft of air keeps the flame flickering without blowing it out. Air cannot be seen. Its presence can be inferred by seeing an object wavering in the wind, or by feeling the movement of air through the sense of touch. The flickering flame implies the presence of air, which is worshipped as the Lord in this temple.

Tiruvannamalai

At Tiruvannamalai *Aruṇācaleśvara* Temple, the Lord is worshipped as *agni*, fire. This temple is dedicated to Lord *Śiva*, known as *Aruṇācaleśvara*, who is believed to have revealed himself here to the *devatās* in the form of light. The *śivaliṅga* in the temple is worshipped as *tejoliṅga*, the fire *liṅga*.

The hill adjacent to the temple is itself seen as a *liṅga*. On the day of *Kṛttikā* star, in the month of *Kārttika* (October - November) a big fire called the Kartikai dipam, the flame of *Kārttika*, is lit on the top of the hill. The fire can be seen from a great distance.

Tirucchirapalli

In the *Jambukeśvara* Temple, located in Tirucchirapalli, the presiding deity is *Śiva* in the form of *Jambuka*. *Jambuka* is one of the names of *Varuṇa*, the presiding deity of water. Here the Lord is worshipped as the element of water.

Kāñcīpuram

In *Kāñcīpuram* about forty kilometers from Chennai, is a *Śiva* temple called the *Ekāmreśvara* Temple, where the Lord is worshipped as the element earth. The *śivaliṅga* in the temple sanctum is made of earth. The name *ekāmra*, meaning 'one mango', refers to a mango tree in the temple that is said to produce only one mango at a time.

EXERCISE

I. Answer these questions:

1. Name the five basic elements in Sanskrit and in English.

2. Explain how each element is seen in the creation of the human body.

3. What is the secret of Chidambaram?

4. Give two names for the presiding deity of water.

5. Explain why the Lord can be invoked in any form.

6. Which two elements do not have a form?

7. The five temples devoted to the elements are Chidambaram, Kalahasti, Tiruvannamalai, Tiruchirapalli and *Kāñcīpuram*. Which element is the deity in each temple?

II. Identify the element that blesses.

1. Seeing the trees sway is a blessing of ____________________.

2. The rains that come are a blessing of ____________________.

3. Having enough room for everyone is a blessing of ____________________.

4. The warmth of the sun is a blessing of ____________________.

5. The plants that grow are a blessing of ____________________.

6. The *prāṇa* that fills your lungs is a blessing of ____________________.

7. The rivers that flow are a blessing of ____________________.

8. The minerals and gems are a blessing of ____________________.

9. The heat in your home is a blessing of ____________________.

10. Winds are a blessing of ____________________.

11. Fossil fuels are a blessing of ____________________.

12. That which accommodates all is a blessing of ____________________.

THREE FORMS OF THE LORD

In the Vedic vision, the Lord is both the intelligent and the material cause of the creation. He is appreciated in the form of various laws and functions as the *trimūrti*. Masculine and feminine aspects of the creation are represented in this vision by denoting the intelligent cause as masculine and the material cause as feminine.

Creation and destruction go together, like two sides of a coin. One cannot exist without the other. In fact, the creation of one object necessarily involves the destruction of another. For example, the creation of a pot-form from a lump of clay involves the destruction of the lump-form. And, between creation and destruction, sustenance of the created object is inevitable. Even though these functions are interdependent, for the sake of worship, the Lord is invoked through each function independently.

From the standpoint of the created universe, the Lord is conceived as having a threefold form, corresponding to three simultaneous functions: creation, sustenance and destruction. He is looked upon as the deities *Brahmā*, *Viṣṇu* and *Rudra* respectively, representing the intelligent aspect of each function. The consorts for these deities are *Sarasvatī*, *Lakṣmī* and *Pārvatī*, respectively. These consorts represent the material aspect of each function.

The Individual Deities

Brahmā

Brahmā is the creator. The word '*Brahmā*' derives from the verbal root '*bṛhi*' meaning 'to grow'. The derivation of the word is "*bṛṃhati, vardhayati yaḥ saḥ Brahmā*" - *Brahmā* is one who causes growth.

In the *Purāṇas*, *Brahmā* is depicted as having four heads. These are said to represent the four directions or the four *Vedas*. *Brahmā* is said to have been born from the navel of Lord *Viṣṇu* at the beginning of the creation.

Sarasvatī

Creation is possible only when one has knowledge of that which is to be created. *Brahmā*, being the creator, is wedded to knowledge. His consort, *Sarasvatī*, represents all forms of knowledge. The word '*Sarasvatī*' means "*saro nīraṃ, jñānaṃ vā, tadvat, raso vā tasyāḥ iti*" - one who possesses water or knowledge, or one who is the essence of everything.

Sarasvatī is depicted in white, holding *vīṇā* in one hand and the *Vedas* in the other. The colour white represents purity. Knowledge is pure when it is unsullied by doubts, errors or vagueness. The *vīṇā* represents the fine and performing arts. The *Vedas* represent all scriptural knowledge.

Viṣṇu

Lord *Viṣṇu* is the sustainer of creation. The word '*Viṣṇu*' means "*vyāpnoti viśvaṃ yaḥ*" - the one who pervades the world. In the process of sustaining the creation, *Viṣṇu* also preserves and pervades the creation. He is also the preserver of *dharma*. The *Purāṇas* describe how Lord *Viṣṇu* manifests in the world to preserve *dharma*, when unrighteousness becomes rampant. The ten manifestations, *avatāras*, of Lord *Viṣṇu* that the *Purāṇas* describe are: *Matsya*, fish; *Kūrma*, tortoise; *Varāha*, boar; *Narasiṃha*, lion-man; *Vāmana*, dwarf; and *Paraśurāma*, *Rāma*, *Kṛṣṇa*, *Buddha* and *Kalki*. *Kalki*, the last *avatāra*, is yet to manifest.

Lord *Viṣṇu* is depicted in a reclining posture asleep on the serpent *Adiśeṣa*. In this posture, he represents the creation in unmanifest form. The coiled serpent, *Adiśeṣa*, symbolises the latent power of creation. When the creation is to become manifest, *Brahmā* arises from *Viṣṇu* and begins the process of creation.

Lakṣmī

Lakṣmī, the consort of Lord *Viṣṇu*, represents wealth and prosperity, the sustaining power of creation. She is ornamented in gold and jewels. The word '*Lakṣmī*' means "*lakṣayati paśyati udyoginam iti*"- the one who can be obtained with diligence and perseverance.

Lakṣmī is manifest in many different forms. The eight forms of *Lakṣmī* that are commonly worshipped are: *Dhanalakṣmī* in the form of wealth; *Dhānyalakṣmī* in the form of grains and crops; *Dhairyalakṣmī* in the form of courage; *Vīryalakṣmī* in the form of valour; *Vijayalakṣmī* in the form of success; *Gajalakṣmī* in the form of sovereignty; *Saubhāgyalakṣmī* in the form of good fortune; and *Vidyalakṣmī* in the form of knowledge.

Rudra or *Śiva*

Rudra is a form of Lord *Śiva*. The word '*Rudra*' means "*sarva-saṃhārakaḥ*" - the one who destroys everything. With reference to the creation, *Rudra* is depicted as the deity of destruction. Lord *Śiva* also has other manifestations. In one form, he is depicted as sitting in meditation. He meditates upon himself as the Lord. He is also depicted as Lord *Dakṣiṇāmūrti*, the first teacher of self-knowledge. In this form, he destroys ignorance of oneself and helps one gain freedom.

Pārvatī

To destroy, one needs power and strength. Lord *Śiva*'s consort, *Pārvatī*, represents strength. This is why she is also called *Śakti*, which means strength. The *Purāṇas* describe *Śiva* and *Pārvatī* as residing in the mountains of *Kailāsa*. The word '*Pārvatī*' is derived as "*parvatānām adhiṣṭhātrī devī*" - the one who is the presiding deity of the mountains or "*parvato himācalas-tasya apatyam*" - the one who is the daughter of (the deity of) the *Himālaya* mountains.

EXERCISE

I. Fill in the blanks with the words below to complete each sentence.

Śiva	purity	wealth	*Śakti*
Vedas	unmanifest	manifest	latent power

1. The four heads of Lord *Brahmā* represent the four ____________.

2. Goddess *Sarasvatī* is adorned in a white sari representing ________________ of knowledge.

3. Lord *Viṣṇu* depicted in a reclining posture represents the creation in the ________________ form.

4. The coiled serpent symbolises the ________________ for creation in the unmanifest.

5. Goddess *Lakṣmī* represents ________________ and prosperity.

6. ________________ is the deity of destruction.

7. Goddess *Pārvatī* is the consort of the Lord of destruction and is also known as ________________.

II. Match the eight names of Goddess *Lakṣmī* with her different forms.

Dhānyalakṣmī	*Vīryalakṣmī*	*Vidyālakṣmī*	*Dhanalakṣmī*
Saubhāgyalakṣmī	*Gajalakṣmī*	*Dhairyalakṣmī*	*Vijayalakṣmī*

1. wealth ____________________
2. knowledge ____________________
3. valour ____________________
4. courage ____________________
5. sovereignty ____________________
6. grains and crops ____________________
7. success ____________________
8. good fortune ____________________

III. Name the consort of each God.

Srīdevī	*Sarasvatī*	*Lakṣmī*
Pārvatī	*Sītā*	*Rukmiṇī*

1. *Śiva* ____________________
2. *Veṅkaṭeśvara* ____________________
3. *Brahmā* ____________________
4. *Kṛṣṇa* ____________________
5. *Viṣṇu* ____________________
6. *Rāma* ____________________

IV. Points to Ponder:

1. From the puranic stories identify two deities who do not have consorts. Describe the birth of both deities and their lives.

   ____

   ____

   ____

2. Do you have a family deity that your family has been worshipping for generations? What is the name of the deity?

   ____

   ____

   ____

IṢṬA DEVATĀS

Īśvara, the Lord, is worshipped from the standpoint of different laws and functions in the form of various deities. As the laws and the functions are countless, *Īśvara* can be worshipped in countless forms. There are, however, some traditional forms for worshipping *Īśvara* which have evolved through the centuries. These deities include *Gaṇeśa*, *Śiva*, *Rāma*, *Kṛṣṇa*, *Durgā*, *Lakṣmī* and *Dakṣiṇāmūrti*.

The deity chosen for worship by a given person, based upon his disposition and liking, is known as *iṣṭa-devatā*. For instance, one who cannot but express one's devotion by singing and dancing may choose Lord *Kṛṣṇa* for worship, while a person with a quiet disposition inclined to spiritual learning may choose Lord *Dakṣiṇāmūrti*. One's own choice can also be determined by a family tradition of worshipping a particular deity. This deity then becomes the *kula-devatā*, the family deity, whose worship is handed down through generations. Sometimes a whole village together worships a particular deity known as the *grāma-devatā*, who also serves as the presiding deity of the village.

One worships the chosen deity, or deities, as the Lord. Most people have an altar for worship, having many gods and goddesses in the form of icons and pictures. One may have his or her primary deity in the centre of the altar and place the other deities around the primary deity.

In the *itihāsas* and the *Purāṇas*, there are different stories told about the various deities. Each deity is depicted with a different form. This form is based on either symbolic representation of the functions the deity represents, or on the mythological stories surrounding its manifestation. A person chooses the form that is most pleasing and cultivates a special relationship with that deity. Some of the popular forms of *iṣṭa-devatās* are discussed below:

Lord *Gaṇeśa*

Lord *Gaṇeśa* is depicted with a form having the body of a human and the head of an elephant. In the mythology, he is the son of Lord *Śiva* and Goddess *Pārvatī*. The word '*Gaṇeśa*' in Sanskrit means Lord of all beings. Some of his other names are *Gajānana*, one who has the face of an elephant; and *Vighneśvara*, the Lord who removes all obstacles.

Gaṇeśa is also considered to be the Lord of wisdom. *Gaṇeśa* has a large forehead which stands for the intellect. His large ears symbolise the importance of listening and learning. The trunk symbolises the discriminative capacity because it is strong enough to carry out heavy tasks, like carrying or uprooting a tree, and at the same time sensitive enough to pick up tiny objects from the ground.

It is important for the intellect to have the capacity for discrimination with regard to the finer issues as well as the bigger issues that one encounters. His large belly represents the presence of the whole universe within him. His form also represents curiosity and memory, two qualities associated with the elephant. Thus the whole form symbolises listening, discrimination, curiosity and memory, all of which are necessary for one to acquire knowledge and wisdom.

When an idol or a picture of *Gaṇeśa* is not available for worship, he is invoked in a lump of turmeric or a betelnut. Once invoked, the form is looked upon as a deity until the worship is over.

A *pūjā* to any deity is begun only after one performs a *pūjā* to Lord *Gaṇeśa*, as he is the remover of all obstacles. One prays to him for the successful completion of the *pūjā*. He is also worshipped on the day of *Gaṇeśa-caturthī*, which falls on the fourth day of the bright half of the lunar month of *Bhādrapada* (August - September).

Śivaliṅga

Īśvara as Lord *Śiva* is generally worshipped in a particular form known as *liṅga*. The word '*liṅga*' in Sanskrit means a symbol. The derivation of the word is "*liṅgyate bhudhyate anena iti liṅgam*" - that by which (something) is represented or known is *liṅga*.

The *liṅga* is a form which has no particular form. If all forms in the creation were put together that would form an indefinable form which is symbolised by the *liṅga*. Since all forms are *Īśvara* and *Īśvara* is not any one form, the *liṅga* represents the formless form of *Īśvara*.

It is believed that a highly symbolic and esoteric philosophy emerged with the advent of *Tantra-yoga*, addressing masculine and feminine principles in the creation. During this time, the *śivaliṅga* came to be looked upon by some people as representing the union of masculine and feminine aspects symbolised as a phallus. However, there is no known reference of such a meaning in the *Vedas*.*

Lord *Śiva* is the deity for those desirous of gaining *mokṣa*, liberation. *Śiva* is commonly worshipped on Mondays. People in North India generally worship Lord *Śiva* by chanting *Śivamahimna-stotra*. Lord *Śiva* is also worshipped on the day and night of *Śivarātri*, a festival which occurs during the month of *Phālguna* (February - March). *Śivarātri* is an important day of prayer and fasting for spiritual seekers.

Śāligrāma

Lord *Viṣṇu* is the sustainer of creation.** He is invoked in a *śāligrāma*, which is a type of stone obtained from the River *Gaṇḍakī* in Nepal. *śāligrāma* is also the name of a sacred place of pilgrimage in the Himalayan ranges where the River *Gaṇḍakī* originates.

This stone contains marks of the *cakra*, disc, a weapon Lord *Viṣṇu* holds in his hand; it gains its importance from its association with Lord *Viṣṇu* as told in the puranic stories. There are nineteen different types of *śāligrāmas*.

Lord *Viṣṇu* is commonly worshipped on the day of *Vāikuṇtha-ekādaśī*, which falls in the month of *Mārgaśira* (November - December) and during *Satyanārāyaṇa-pūjā* , which is performed on the full moon day every month.

Lord *Rāma* and *Kṛṣṇa*

Lord *Viṣṇu* is also worshipped in the form of his incarnations, such as Lord *Rāma* and Lord *Kṛṣṇa*. People in the Vedic culture look upon them as *avatāras*, incarnations of *Īśvara*. *Īśvara* does not exist apart from the creation and has the capacity to manifest in the creation in any particular form. It is believed that this manifestation happens as a result of people's prayers during the times when unrighteousness prevails. An *avatāra* re-establishes *dharma*, thus blessing humanity. As Lord *Kṛṣṇa* says in the *Bhagavad Gītā* (4.7):

यदा यदा हि धर्मस्य ग्लानिर्भवति भारत ।
अभ्युत्थानम् अधर्मस्य तदात्मानं सृजाम्यहम् ॥

yadā yadā hi dharmasya glānirbhavati bhārata
abhyutthānam adharmasya tadātmānaṃ sṛjāmyaham

yadā yadā - whenever; *hi* - indeed; *dharmasya* - of right living; *glāniḥ* - decline; *bhavati* - is; *bhārata* - O *Arjuna*; *abhyutthānam* - rise everywhere; *adharmasya* - of wrong living; *tadā* - then; *ātmānam*- myself; *sṛjāmi* - bring into being (assume a physical body); *aham* - I

"O *Arjuna*, whenever there is a decline in right living, and an increase in wrong living everywhere, I bring myself into being (assume a physical body)."

Invoking and worshipping *Īśvara* in various forms, animate and inanimate, is unique to the Vedic culture. These symbolisms are abstract and are based upon an understanding and vision of the Lord.

Pārvatī, *Lakṣmī* and *Sarasvatī*

Goddess *Pārvatī*, Goddess *Lakṣmī* and Goddess *Sarasvatī* are worshipped during *Navarātri* or *Daśarā* which is celebrated in the month of *Āśvina* (September - October). This festival lasts for nine days. *Pārvatī*, in the form of *Durgā*, is worshipped during the first three days. In this form she is said to have destroyed the demon *Mahiśāsura*. During the next three days Goddess *Lakṣmī* is worshipped by those who seek prosperity and wealth. *Lakṣmī* is also worshipped during *Dīpāvali* festival.

During the last three days of *Navarātri* Goddess *Sarasvatī* is worshipped. On the ninth day an altar is made of books, instruments of fine and performing arts and implements of various professions, all of which represent knowledge and skill. At this altar Goddess *Sarasvatī* is invoked and worshipped.

Other Forms of Worship

The Lord is worshipped in many other forms, including the cow, the elephant, the trees and the rivers. These forms serve as vehicles for invoking *Īśvara* due to their importance in the lives of the people, their associations with the various deities in the *Purāṇas*, and their symbolic representations. Worship of *Īśvara* in many forms reflects an appreciation of the knowledge that the world does not exist apart from him.

Cow Worship

In the Vedic culture the cow has gained special significance. The cow was a significant asset to people in the Vedic society who primarily lived an agrarian life. Taking very little, in the form of hay and grass, the cow provided the family with milk products and other by-products. She also brought prosperity to the family, whose wealth was measured by the number of cows and other animals they possessed.

The cow is associated with the life of Lord *Kṛṣṇa*, who grew up as a cowherd. There are stories in the *Purāṇas* about *Kāmadhenu*, the wish-fulfilling celestial cow. Giving away cows in charity is an important step in many Vedic rituals.

On the day after the Pongal festival, which falls in the month of January, the cow is worshipped and thanked for her role in the lives of the people.

Elephant Worship

The elephant brings to mind the form of Lord *Gaṇeśa*. The elephant is also a great worker in the South India, where it is utilised in the timber and lumber industries. The *Purāṇas* tell the story of *Gajendra-mokṣa*, the release of elephant *Gajendra* who was a great devotee of Lord *Viṣṇu*.Various other animals are associated with deities. For example, the bull with Lord *Śiva*; the peacock with Lord *Subrahmaṇya*; and the tiger with Goddess *Durgā*.

***Tulaśī* Worship**

The *tulaśī* plant is seen as the manifestation of Goddess *Lakṣmī*. It is known for its medicinal and healing qualities. There are many stories associated with *tulaśī* in the *Viṣṇu Purāṇa* and in the *Devī Bhāgavata*. In many Indian households there is a *tulaśī* plant in the backyard which is worshipped every morning.

Yantra and Tantra Worship

Yantra and *tantra* are highly symbolic and esoteric forms of invoking the Lord. *Yantras* are instruments and visual symbols representing the various deities and other aspects of creation. The *Śrī - Yantra*, also known as the *Śrī-cakra*, is looked upon as symbolic of the whole creation.

Tantra is a particular system of worship involving elaborate esoteric rituals based on the tantric philosophy. There are two main forms of *tantra* worship seen in India. *Vāmatantra* is practised in Kashmir and Bengal; and a variation of it, called *Dakṣiṇamārga*, is observed in Kerala.

* Refer to "*Vedas*", Puranic Encyclopedia.

** Refer to "Three forms of the Lord", Part 7.

✍ EXERCISE ✍

I. True or False. *Check one.*

1. The deity that one likes to worship is called *iṣṭa-devatā*. [T] [F]

2. There are no traditional forms of worship. [T] [F]

3. The deities are brought to life in the *itihāsas* and *purāṇas*. [T] [F]

4. One cannot invoke the Lord in any form. [T] [F]

5. Lord *Gaṇeśa* is worshipped at the end of every *pūjā*. [T] [F]

6. Most Indian homes have a *pūjā* room. [T] [F]

7. The *śāligrāma* stone gains its importance from its association with Lord *Viṣṇu*. [T] [F]

8. In the *Vedas*, it is said that the *śivaliṅga* represents the union of masculine and feminine aspects [T] [F]

9. An *avatāra* is a manifestation of the Lord in a particular form. [T] [F]

10. Families no longer worship family deities, called *kula-devatās*. [T] [F]

II. Fill in the blanks with the words below to appreciate the form of Lord *Gaṇeśa*.

forehead	large ears	tail
large belly	whole elephant form	trunk

1. Lord *Gaṇeśa's* ________________ symbolises the intellect.

2. His ________________ symbolise the importance of listening to the scriptures.

3. His ________________ symbolises the discriminative capacity.

4. His ________________ symbolises the whole universe is within him.

5. His ________________ symbolises the memory.

III. Answer these questions:

1. What is a *liṅga*?

2. Name four forms in which the Lord is worshipped.

3. Name two *iṣṭa-devatās* that are commonly worshipped.

4. Why is the cow worshipped in India?

IV. Points to Ponder:

1. Do Hindus worship many Gods, or only God? Explain.

2. Who is your *iṣṭa-devatā*? How did you choose this deity?

3. Why do different people have different *iṣṭa-devatās*?

THE PLANETARY DEITIES

Invoking the Lord in the form of planetary deities is one of the unique forms of worshipping *Īśvara* seen in the Vedic culture. The planetary deities are perceived as playing a significant role in the life of an individual. *Jyotiṣa*, one of the *Vedāṅgas*, includes astronomy and astrology. *Jyotiṣa* connects the life events of a human being to the orderly patterns of the movements of the planets in the earth's solar system.*

In addition, astrology is a predictive science based upon the positions of the various planets cast at the time of one's birth (the horoscope). While the horoscope indicates the life pattern destined at birth, the law of *karma* enables an individual, within the confines of his birth, to exercise free will through actions and to change destined events. These actions include prayers known as *śānti*.

Śāntis are specific prayers offered to *Īśvara* who is invoked in the form of various planetary deities called *grahas*. *Jyotiṣa* recognises nine planets, *nava-grahas*, that are associated with various life experiences. These planetary deities also preside over the twelve signs of the zodiac in the following order: Aries, Taurus, Gemini, Cancer, Leo, Virgo, Libra, Scorpio, Sagittarius, Capricorn, Aquarius and Pisces.

Navagraha Devatās

Sūrya Devatā

Because the essential nature of *Sūrya*, the sun, is light, it is called the *ātmakāraka* or the presiding deity of the *ātmā*, awareness. The sun governs a person's confidence, authority and status. The sun is also the presiding deity of the eyes and rules the sign Leo. The *Viṣṇu Purāṇa* (2.8.15) states that the sun does not move; nor does it rise or set. Rising and setting imply appearance and disappearance.

Candra *Devatā*

Candra, the moon, is the presiding deity of the mind and emotions. This *devatā* is depicted with crescent moon, holding lotus buds in his hands. He rules the sign of Cancer.

Kuja *Devatā*

The deity *Kuja*, the Mars, is also known as *Maṅgala* or *Aṅgāraka*. In the *Purāṇas* he is also described as *Kārtikeya*, the son of Lord *Śiva* and Goddess *Pārvatī*. He is depicted as wearing red clothes and carrying a spear. He governs the qualities of courage and bravery, and presides over siblings and health. He rules Aries and Scorpio.

Budha *Devatā*

Budha, the Mercury, is the deity who presides over intelligence. He governs a person's teaching capacities. He is depicted as holding the *Vedas* in one hand and a sword, a mace and a shield in his other hands. He rules Gemini and Virgo.

Guru *Devatā*

Guru, the Jupiter, is the presiding deity of religious inclinations and prosperity. He is also the presiding deity of married life for women. He is described in the *Purāṇas* as *Bṛhaspati*, the preceptor of the *devatās*. He is often depicted in a standing posture with four hands, in one of which he holds a weapon called the *vajra-āyudha*. He rules Sagittarius and Pisces.

Śukra Devatā

Śukra, the Venus, is the presiding deity of material comforts, arts, culture and aesthetics. He is also the presiding deity of love and married life for men. In the *Purāṇas* he is depicted as being the preceptor of King *Bali*. *Śukra* is depicted as standing with his hands folded. He is the ruler of Taurus and Libra.

Śani Devatā

Śani, the Saturn is the presiding deity of longevity, calamities and difficulties in life and at the same time, of renunciation and spiritual wisdom. He presides over painful experiences and inner growth. In the *Purāṇas*, he is considered the son of the sun deity. He is depicted with a dark complexion, bearing a mace and moving at a slow pace. He has a crow as his vehicle. His eyes are generally blind-folded because of the belief that his glance is very powerful and may bring misfortune. He rules Capricorn and Aquarius.

Rāhu and *Ketu Devatās*

Rāhu is the presiding deity of worldly desires and *Ketu* is the presiding deity of *mokṣa*, or freedom from limitations. Astronomically, they are not planets but the northern and southern nodal points of the moon. They are closely connected to each other astrologically. Mythologically, they are born of a *rākṣasa*. The upper half of *Rāhu's* body is similar to a man, while the lower half is like a snake. Conversely, the upper half of *Ketu's* body is similar to the head of a snake, while the lower half is like a man. They do not rule any signs but give the effects of the ruler of the signs where they are situated.

In many Indian temples, there is an altar dedicated to the nine planetary *devatās*. They are placed in the following manner, facing specific directions as pointed by the arrows

		North		
	Ketu	*Guru*	*Budha*	
West	*Śani*	*Surya*	*Śukra*	**East**
	Rāhu	*Kuja*	*Candra*	
		South		

Before leaving the temple one offers prayers to these deities by circumambulating nine times around the altar, while chanting the *Navagraha-stotras*, or the following prayer:

आरोग्यं प्रददातु नो दिनकरः चन्द्रो यशो निर्मलं भूतिं भूमिसुतः सुधांशुतनयः प्रज्ञां गुरुर्गौरवम् ।
काव्यः कोमलवाग्विलासमतुलं मन्दो मुदं सर्वदा राहुर्बाहुबलं विरोधशमनं केतुः कुलस्योन्नतिम् ॥

ārogyaṃ pradadātu na dinakaraḥ candro yaśo nirmalam
bhūtim bhūmisutaḥ sudhāṃśutanayaḥ prajñāṃ gururgauravam
kāvyaḥ komalavāgvilāsamatulaṃ mando mudaṃ sarvadā
rāhurbāhubalaṃ virodhaśamanaṃ ketuḥ kulasyonnatim

ārogyam - long life and good health; *pradadātu* - may give; *naḥ* - us; *dinakaraḥ* - the sun; *candraḥ* - moon; *yaśaḥ* - fame; *nirmalam* - pure; *bhūtim* - charisma and prosperity; *bhūmisutaḥ* - Mars, the son of earth; *sudhāmśu-tanayaḥ* - Mercury, the son of moon; *prajñām* - intelligence; *gururḥ* - Jupiter; *gauravam* - respectability; *kāvyaḥ* - Venus, the one possessed of the quality of a poet; *komala-vāgvilāsam* - capacity for melodious speech; *atulam* - unsurpassed; *mandaḥ* - Saturn, the one of slow gait; *mudam* - joy and pleasure; *sarvadā* - always; *rāhuḥ* - *Rāhu*; *bāhubalam* - strength; *virodha-śamanam* - destruction of enemies; *ketuḥ* - *Ketu*; *kulasya* - of the family; *unnatim* - the growth

"May the Sun give us long life and good health; the Moon, pure fame; Mars, the son of Earth, charisma and prosperity; Mercury, the son of the Moon, intelligence; Jupiter, respectability; Venus, the one possessed of the qualities of a poet, the capacity for unsurpassed and elegant speech; Saturn, the one of slow gait, continual joy and pleasure; *Rāhu*, strength and the destruction of enemies; and *Ketu*, growth of the family."

* Refer to "Astronomy and Astrology", Part 11.

EXERCISE

I. Fill in the blanks with the words below to complete each sentence.

prayers	planets	stars
Astrology	Astronomy	horoscope

1. _________________ is the study of the movement of the planets in the universe.

2. _________________ is a predictive science based on astronomy.

3. A _________________ indicates a pattern of life destined at the time of birth of an individual.

4. *Śāntis* are _________________ performed to seek the blessings of the Lord in averting unforeseen and undesirable events.

5. The Lord is invoked in the form of nine _________________ which are associated with different aspects of life experience.

II. Match the planets with the signs they rule.

Sagittarius and Pisces

Capricorn and Aquarius

Gemini and Virgo

Taurus and Libra

Leo

Aries and Scorpio

Cancer

1. Sun ______________________________

2. Venus ______________________________

3. Moon ______________________________

4. Saturn ______________________________

5. Jupiter ______________________________

6. Mars ______________________________

7. Mercury ______________________________

III. Complete each sentence.

health	eyes	*mokṣa*	mind
love	wisdom	marriage	spiritual pursuit

1. The sun is the deity of the ____________________.

2. The moon is the deity of the ____________________.

3. Mars is the deity of ____________________.

4. Jupiter is the deity of ____________________.

5. As *Bṛhaspati*, Jupiter is the deity of ____________________.

6. Venus is the deity of ____________________.

7. Saturn is the deity of calamities and ____________________.

8. *Rāhu* is the deity of worldly desires, while *Ketu* is the deity of ____________________.

LORD *DAKṢIṆĀMŪRTI*

Lord *Dakṣiṇāmūrti* is Lord *Śiva* manifest as the first teacher. It is said in the *Purāṇas* that in the beginning of creation Lord *Brahmā*, the creator, created out of his mind four progenies known as the *Sānatkumāras*: *Sanaka*, *Sanandana*, *Sanatkumāra* and *Sanatsujāta*. It is said that Lord *Brahmā* asked them to join him in the task of creation. However, they were renunciates by nature and even at a young age, possessed a keen desire to know the truth. The *Sānatkumāras* set out in the northern direction in search of truth.

They performed great penance to please the Lord. Lord *Śiva* appeared before them in the form of *Dakṣiṇāmūrti* and imparted self-knowledge to the *Sānatkumāras*. It is said that Lord *Dakṣiṇāmūrti* in silent exposition revealed the truth, which is the identity between the individual and *Brahman*, the limitless. This identity is revealed by a symbolic hand gesture called the *cinmudrā* or *jñāna-mudrā*.

The Word *Dakṣiṇā*

The word '*dakṣiṇā*' means south and the word '*mūrti*' means form. *Dakṣiṇāmūrti* means the form which is facing south. The Lord is depicted as teaching while facing the southern direction. The students, on the other hand, face north. The Sanskrit word for north is *uttara*, which means 'to rise and cross over'. This direction symbolises the human quest for overcoming limitations and gaining *mokṣa*, liberation. Therefore, the disciples are facing north. The south, on the other hand, is associated with ignorance and death. The teacher faces south because he is enlightened and has conquered death.

Ever Young

We are told of the wonder that under the banyan tree sits the teacher who is ever young surrounded by disciples who are old. *Dakṣiṇāmūrti* is ever young because the self never ages. He is beyond time and therefore free from birth and death and other modifications implied by time. He is of the nature of *ānanda*, fullness, which is manifest in his pleasing countenance. His disciples are depicted as old. Taking themselves to be the body, they are subject to repeated cycles of birth and death from beginningless time. Their age also symbolises emotional maturity, an important qualification in the pursuit of self-knowledge.

The Form

Lord *Dakṣiṇāmūrti* represents the first teacher of spiritual knowledge. In the *śāstra*, he is given a particular form for the purpose of worship and contemplation. There are many features in this form and a certain meaning is associated with each of them.

Lord *Dakṣiṇāmūrti* has four hands. In his lower right hand, he exhibits the *cinmudrā* and also holds a *Japa-mālā*. In his upper right hand, the Lord is holding a *damaru*, a small drum. In his upper left hand we see fire, and in the lower left hand, a book. The sun and the moon adorn the crown of the Lord. We also see in his matted locks a maiden figure representing the *Gaṅgā*. In his right ear, the Lord wears a man's ear-ring, and in his left ear, a woman's ear-ring. He is adorned with necklaces and armlets, a belt and bracelets. His left foot is resting on his right thigh, in the posture called *vīrāsana* and his right foot presses a dwarf-like crouching demon called *Apasmāra*. Some of the features, such as the silent exposition, the *cinmudrā*, the book, the banyan tree and the demon *Apasmāra* are peculiar to the *Dakṣiṇāmūrti* form, while the rest of the features are associated with Lord *Śiva* in general.

Lord *Śiva* is the substratum upon which the play of the creation, sustenance and destruction of the universe takes place. The *ḍamaru*, the small drum, symbolises creation, whereas fire stands for destruction. The *śāstra* describes the whole cosmos as the body of the Lord with heaven as his head, earth as his feet and the sun and the moon as his eyes. The various ornaments represent the glories of the Lord.

The entire form represents the Lord as the creation which is made up of the five basic elements: space, air, fire, water and earth. The drum, which produces sound, stands for the element space. His matted locks held together by a bandanna, or band represent air. Space and air being invisible to the eye, their presence is inferred by these symbols. Fire is shown in one hand in the form of a torch and water is represented by the *Gaṅgā* flowing from his head. Earth is represented by the whole form and also by the ashes smeared on the body of the Lord.

The banyan tree represents *saṃsāra*, or the limitations of worldly existence, a commonly used metaphor in the scriptures. However, *saṃsāra* has its reality in *Brahman* which is the root and therefore Lord *Dakṣiṇāmūrti* is shown as seated at the root of the tree.

The bull on which the Lord rides stands for *dharma*, justice and virtue. His name is *Nandikeśvara*, the Lord of joy; or *Nandi*, meaning, joyful. He is a great devotee of Lord *Śiva* and according to the *Purāṇas*, he is said to have performed a great penance at a place called *Uttaramayūra-kṣetra*. Lord *Śiva*, pleased with his penance, appeared before him in the form of *Dakṣiṇāmūrti* and taught him. *Nandikeśvara* is considered to be one of the *ācāryas* of Saivism.

Lord *Śiva* is said to be *Ardhanārīśvara*, half male and half female, representing the intelligent cause and the material cause of the creation, respectively. This union is symbolically represented in Lord *Dakṣiṇāmūrti* who wears a male ear-ring in the right ear and a female ear-ring in the left ear.

The book in his lower left hand stands for knowledge, the Lord being the source of all knowledge. He also has a *Japa-mālā* which is employed for repeating a *mantra*. The Sanskrit alphabet consists of fifty-four letters. Repeated forward and backward, the total is 108. The alphabet is that from which all speech and therefore all *mantras* have evolved. The *Japa-mālā*, which has 108 beads, therefore, represents the garland of letters and is called *akṣa-mālā*. The *Japa-mālā* also represents all spiritual disciplines.

The demon who is shown under the right foot of the Lord is called *Apasmāra*. *Apasmāra* stands for the ego which is a product of self-ignorance. Lord *Dakṣiṇāmūrti* has the demon under his foot showing that in the wake of self-knowledge the ego is subdued.

The form of Lord *Dakṣiṇāmūrti* discussed above is called *Medhā Dakṣiṇāmūrti*. The word '*medhā*' means knowledge. Some of the other forms of Lord *Dakṣiṇāmūrti* include *Yoga Dakṣiṇāmūrti*, in which he is shown seated in the *yoga* posture; and *Vīṇā Dakṣiṇāmūrti*, where he is shown holding a *vīṇā* in two hands.

Every traditional *Śiva* temple has, to the right of the sanctum, an altar for Lord *Dakṣiṇāmūrti*. Special worship is performed on *Dakṣiṇāmūrti-jayanti*, which falls on the eleventh day of the bright half of the lunar cycle in the month of *Caitra* (March-April).

EXERCISE

I. Circle the correct answer.

1. Under what tree does Lord *Dakṣiṇāmūrti* sit?
   a) pipal
   b) banyan
   c) margosa

2. What is Lord *Dakṣiṇāmūrti's* vehicle?
   a) tiger
   b) peacock
   c) bull

3. Lord *Dakṣiṇāmūrti* is a form of
   a) *Śiva*
   b) *Viṣṇu*
   c) *Kālī*

4. Which river flows from the Lord's matted locks?
   a) *Yamunā*
   b) *Kāverī*
   c) *Gaṅgā*

5. What is the name of the demon under his right foot?
   a) *Muyalaka*
   b) *Apasmāra*
   c) *Apsarā*

6. What does this demon represent?
   a) ego
   b) *adharma*
   c) desire

7. Which two objects adorn his head?
   a) the sun and the stars
   b) the sun and the moon
   c) the moon and the stars

8. *Dakṣiṇāmūrti* is looked upon as the Lord in the form of
   a) an ascetic
   b) an upholder of *dharma*
   c) a teacher of spiritual knowledge

II. Answer these questions:

1. What are the four objects that Lord *Dakṣiṇāmūrti* holds in his hands?

2. What does each object in his hand represent?

3. What are the five aspects of the form of the Lord that represent the five elements?

4. What does *ardhanārīśvara* mean?

5. What direction does Lord *Dakṣiṇāmūrti* face? Why?

6. What are the names of Lord *Dakṣiṇāmūrti's* four disciples?

III. Points to Ponder:

1. Lord *Dakṣiṇāmūrti* is depicted with a serene smile on his face. What do you think the Lord's inner smile means?

____

____

____

____

____

2. Why is it appropriate to have the Lord represented as a teacher?

____

____

____

____

____

IV. Field Work

Visit the Lord *Dakṣiṇāmūrti* Temple at Anaikkatti, Coimbatore (T.N.), India or Saylorsburg, Pennsylvania, U.S.A. Find out if there are any other temples devoted to Lord *Dakṣiṇāmūrti* in India or in America. Why did Arsha Vidya Gurukulam choose *Dakṣiṇāmūrti* as the deity for its temple?

____

____

____

____

THE SYMBOL WORSHIP OF *ĪŚVĀRA*

The Lord, as revealed by scriptures, is non-separate form the creation. When the whole creation is Lord, every form in the creation is the Lord's form. When one is unable to see this fact, it becomes necessary to have the *bhāvanā*, attitude of *bhagavad-buddhi* in a given form. For this purpose, one invokes the Lord in an idol. The tradition has handed down the generations, specific forms and the *bhagavad-buddhi* - seeing any form as the Lord - is associated with those forms in one's mind.

For generations, the Lord has been worshipped in certain forms and those forms have been coming down for generations, which is a great blessing. The tradition did not just begin yesterday. When one sees Lord *Gaṇeśa*, one recognises the form as the Lord, not as a strange creature with an odd head and a big belly. This is what is known as tradition, *sampradāya*. One should understand this as a treasure.

Through this tradition, one is fortunate to have inherited this particular legacy of forms without any effort on one's part. The idol invokes in everyone the devotee and that is a great heritage.

When a person worships, he is not worshipping an idol. Everybody worships the Lord. The sculptors who make the idol do not look upon the idol as a stone or marble, once the Lord is invoked in it. To quote an instance: once an idol of Lord *Śiva* was supplied by a sculptor to a temple. Certain parts of the idol - the eye lashes, the lips, the snake etc., - were colour-painted by the sculptor. In course of some five or six years, the painting got erased. The manager of the temple wrote to the sculptor asking him repaint the idol. The latter replied that he could not paint the Lord. He agreed to make another idol, but not paint the existing one. Why should he refuse, if he only created a statue, an idol and not the Lord?

Only until the installation ceremony, the idol is a stone and not the Lord. During installation, *prāṇa-pratiṣṭhā* - imparting life to the idol - is done by *mantras*, by *saṃskāra*. It is like how a person is made a twice-born through *saṃskāra*. By the *dīkṣā* of *Gayatrī-mantra*, he is made a different person. Similarly, here, even though it is a stone idol, it is given life by *saṃskāra* and the last act of the sculptor is to open the eyes. He brings a fine chisel and a hammer with him and when the *saṃskāras* are done, he opens the eyes of the idol. Till then, the eyes are covered. The sculptor removes bits of stone covering the eyes. And then he is the first person to fall at the feet of the idol which is no more a stone for him. Now it is the Lord and he worships the Lord.

One does not even need a stone for worship. Even in a lump of turmeric powder, one can invoke Lord *Gaṇapati* before beginning a *pūjā* . In a bucket of water, one can invoke all the deities of holy rivers everyday and bathe in the *Gaṅgā*, *Yamunā* and so on - one need not go to these rivers. All that is required is the attitude.

The depth of attitude behind a symbol is experienced very well in our day-to-day life. For instance, when one stands before the picture of one's departed father, what is in front is just a black and white photograph. When a person places a flower there, his offering is not to the piece of paper, but is a mark of respect to his father. Without such forms of expressions of respect, of friendship, of love, life will be void.

Why do people worship the Lord? - one may ask. One cannot ask why people worship the idols. Because one never worships idols but the Lord. One worships the Lord, as it brings about *antaḥkaraṇa-śuddhi*, purity of mind, which is needed to understand that the Lord is everywhere. For this purpose, a person seeks the Lord's grace by worship, which is an action, an act of devotion.

Until one knows that the Lord is everywhere, one has to keep one's ego under check. In fact, the Lord being everything, this ego is swallowed by the Lord. Since one thinks one is different from the Lord, one places a flower at the feet of the Lord and one's ego is kept under check. A symbol, such as an idol, plays an important role in this worship.

EXERCISE

I. Answer the following questions:

1. Why does one invoke the Lord in an idol?

2. Does one worship an idol?

3. Why did the painter refuse to repaint the idol?

4. Why do people worship the Lord?

II. Match the word with its meaning by placing the number of the word in the correct blank.

1.	*Prāṇa pratiṣṭhā*	_____ Purity of the mind
2.	*Bhagavad-buddhi*	_____ Tradition
3.	*Sampradāya*	_____ Religious purification
4.	*Saṃskāra*	_____ Seeing Lord in any form
5.	*Antaḥkaraṇa-suddhi*	_____ Imparting life to the idol

III. Points to Ponder:

a. When you salute the national flag, do you just respect a piece of cloth or is there something more? Compare with idol worship.

____

____

____

____

b. When you see the form of *Gaṇeśa*, you immediately think of Lord. How did this connection come about? See the role of ancestors in this connection.

____

____

____

____

DEVOTION

The Sanskrit word '*bhakti*' means devotion. It is derived from the verbal root '*bhaj*' meaning 'to serve'. *Bhakti* is an act of service done wholeheartedly and without self interest for a person one reveres. There are different types of *bhakti*, depending upon the person one serves: *mātṛ-bhakti*, service to one's mother; *pitṛ-bhakti*, service to one's father; *ācārya-bhakti*, service to one's teacher; *rāja-bhakti*, service to the king; *deva-bhakti*, service to the deities; and *Īśvara -bhakti*, service to the Lord. The term *bhakti* generally refers to one's devotion to the Lord. In *Vivekacūḍāmaṇi* (verse 31) *Ādi Śaṅkara* defines devotion as "*svasvarūpa-anusandhānam*" - contemplation upon the essential nature of the self. Thus, the word '*bhakti*', in the ultimate sense, reveals the identity of oneself with the Lord.

In relating to the world, every individual assumes many roles. A person may assume the role of a father, a son, a husband, a citizen, depending upon the person he is relating to in a given situation. The roles continue to exist as long as the individuals or the objects that evoke the roles exist. For instance, when a man is talking to his son, the father in him emerges. Later, when he talks to his wife the husband emerges, and when he gets a call from his boss, the father and the husband give way to the employee. Thus the roles keep changing and each role is distinct from the others.

Among all the roles one plays, there is one role that can be considered fundamental and universal; a role which applies to every person. This is the relationship of the individual to the total, of the created to the creator, or in other words, of the individual to the Lord. Enquiring into this fundamental relationship, one finds it to be a relationship that does not come and go. The one who relates to the Lord with devotion becomes a devotee. It is this underlying devotee that becomes the father, the son, the husband and the employee.

If one takes the devotee to be a role like any other role, then the devotee may be evoked only in certain situations or at certain times. However, when one understands the invariable relationship between the devotee and the Lord, then it is this basic devotee that is always evoked and abides in the various roles played by the individual.

Types of Devotion

To discover a fundamental relationship with the Lord, one must first discover the devotee within oneself. Prayers, worship, rituals and study of the scriptures are different means by which one comes to discover the devotee in oneself and by which the occasional devotee is transformed into an abiding one. Traditionally nine types of *bhakti* are described:

1) *Śravaṇa* is listening to stories that exemplify the glories of the Lord, such as the *itihāsas* and the *Purāṇas*. *Śravaṇa* also means listening to the scriptural statements that reveal the identity between oneself and the Lord. In the *Bhāgavata* it is said that King *Parīkṣit* heard the glories of the Lord as his mother listened to them while he was in her womb. As a result, later in his life he became a great devotee of the Lord.

2) *Kīrtana* is praising the glories of the Lord by means of devotional songs. In Indian mythology, Sage *Nārada* is presented as a great devotee of Lord *Viṣṇu* who travelled among all the worlds singing the Lord's glories and inspiring men, gods and celestials. It was *Nārada*'s devotion that helped him gain self-knowledge from *Sanatkumāra*. Mirabai, a great devotee of Lord *Kṛṣṇa*, also expressed her love for the Lord through many devotional songs.

3) *Smaraṇa* is constantly remembering the Lord in the form of prayer, *Japa*, or contemplation. *Prahlāda* was a great devotee of the Lord and constantly remembered his name. His father, who was a demon king by the name of *Hiraṇyakaśipu* could not tolerate *Prahlāda*'s devotion to the Lord. *Prahlāda* was protected by the Lord on many occasions when his father attempted to kill him. Eventually the Lord took the incarnation of Lord *Narasiṃha* and killed the demon king.

4) *Padasevana* is serving at the feet of the Lord. This refers to performing various activities of worship with an attitude of humility. Offering worship at the feet of the Lord is an act of devotion and reflects one's humility since the feet are the lowest part of the body. In the *Mahābhārata*, *Vidura* symbolises this attitude of devotion when he welcomes Lord *Kṛṣṇa* to his home by offering worship at his feet.

5) *Arcana* is worship by offering flowers while chanting various names of the Lord. This act of worship is done while performing Vedic rituals and *pūjās*. In the *Purāṇas* and *itihāsas*, kings and *ṛṣis* are seen to offer worship in the form of *arcana* to the Lord.

6) *Vandana* is adoration by offering various forms of salutations to the Lord. *Akrūra* was the uncle of Lord *Kṛṣṇa* and the commander-in-chief of the *Yādava* army. He was known for his adoration and devotion to Lord *Kṛṣṇa* expressed through salutations. It is said that *Akrūra's* devotion was so great that he would salute even the places where Lord *Kṛṣṇa* walked.

7) *Dāsya* is service. In this form of devotion, one spends time performing actions in service of the Lord. *Hanumān* exemplifies service to Lord *Rāma*. From the time he met *Rāma* he served him with devotion and dedication.

8) *Sakhya* is expressing one's devotion to the Lord with the attitude of friendship. This means that one looks upon the Lord as a friend, as did King *Sugrīva* in the *Rāmāyaṇa*.

9) *Ātma-nivedana* is surrendering oneself totally to the Lord. King *Mahābali* offered himself to the Lord by asking Lord *Vāmana* to place his foot on *Mahābali's* head; symbolising surrender of his ego to the Lord.

Types of Devotees

A devotee may express devotion in one or many ways depending upon his disposition. In the *Bhagavad Gītā* (7.16) Lord *Kṛṣṇa* describes four types of devotees:

चतुर्विधा भजन्ते मां जनाः सुकृतिनोऽर्जुन।
आर्तो जिज्ञासुरर्थार्थी ज्ञानी च भरतर्षभ॥

caturvidhā bhajante māṃ janāḥ sukṛtino'rjuna
ārto jijñāsurarthārtī jñānī ca bharatarṣabha

caturvidhāḥ - four types; *bhajante* - worship; *mām* - me; *janāḥ* - people; *sukṛtinaḥ* - virtuous; *arjuna* - O *Arjuna*; *ārtaḥ* - one who is distressed; *jijñāsuḥ*- seeker of knowledge; *arthārtī* - seeker of wealth; *jñānī* - wise person; *ca* - and; *Bharatarṣabha* - O one who is great among the lineage of *Bharata*

"O *Arjuna*, the great among the descendants of *Bharata*, four types of virtuous people worship me; the one who is distressed, the seeker of knowledge, the seeker of wealth and the wise person."

An *ārta* is one type of devotee who worships and remembers the Lord during times of distress. When such a person is helpless and finds no means of dealing with a painful or difficult situation, he or she turns to the Lord. Such a person is considered a devotee as he thinks of the Lord and takes refuge in him. *Draupadī* sought refuge in the Lord when the *Kauravas* attempted to disrobe her in the presence of the *Pāṇḍavas* and the royal family.

A *jijñāsu* is another type of devotee who has a desire for self-knowledge. This person has only one goal in life which is total freedom from limitations. He has discerned that the means to this freedom lies in the discovery of one's identity with the Lord. He does not use the Lord to gain limited ends. His prayers and devotions are meant only to fulfill the goal of gaining self-knowledge. The *Kaṭha Upaniṣad* presents young *Naciketas* as a seeker of self-knowledge. When Lord *Yama* tempts *Naciketas* with worldly and heavenly pleasures, *Naciketas* points out their limitations and requests that Lord *Yama* teach him self-knowledge.

A third type of devotee is an *arthārthī*, a person whose devotion is governed by a desire to achieve various ends, such as wealth, power, name and possessions. Such a person recognises the element of chance in any undertaking and asks for the grace of the Lord in the fulfillment of various desires. *Rāvaṇa* was a great devotee of Lord *Śiva*. He sought to be the most powerful in the three worlds by pleasing the Lord through penance.

The *jñānī*, the fourth type of devotee, is a wise person who has gained the knowledge of the identity between himself and the Lord. His devotion is merely an expression of his appreciation of the presence of the Lord in every being. This is the highest form of devotion and the culmination of all human pursuits. In praising the *jñānī*, Lord *Kṛṣṇa* says in the *Bhagavad Gītā* (7.18): "*jñānī tu ātmaiva me matam*" - I regard the wise person as my very self. In the *Rāmāyaṇa*, King *Janaka* was considered to be a wise person; his decisions as a king were seen as spontaneous expressions of his wisdom.

Bhakti is described in *Nārada-bhakti-sūtra* as "*asmin parama-prema-rūpā*" - an ardent love with reverence for the Lord. *Prema* means love for someone or something. *Paramaprema* is an ardent love combined with reverence. *Bhakti* involves both love and reverence. One can love anything even a cat or a rat. However this is not *bhakti*. In *bhakti*, the object of love is also revered. Generally one does not say that one loves the Lord, but that one is devoted to the Lord.

It is very difficult, if not impossible, to love and revere something that is unknown. It is necessary to understand the Lord as the cause of the entire creation, including oneself. A wise person appreciates the Lord, not only as the cause, but as non-separate from himself. Just as a wave is born of the ocean, is sustained by it and resolves back into it, so also an individual is born of the Lord, sustained by the Lord and resolves back into the Lord. Just as the wave never really exists apart from the ocean, an individual, though seemingly distinct, never exists apart from the Lord. It is in such an understanding that *parama-prema-rūpā bhakti* finds its fulfillment.

EXERCISE

I. Fill in the blanks with the words below to show how each devotee worshipped the Lord.

singing	service	praying
listening	friendship	remembering

1. *Prahlāda* worshipped the Lord by ________________ him.

2. *Hanumān* worshipped the Lord by doing ________________ to him.

3. King *Parīkṣit* worshipped the Lord by ________________ to his glories.

4. Mirabai worshipped the Lord by ________________ his glories.

5. *Sudāmā* worshipped the Lord by discovering a ________________ with the Lord.

II. **Classify the devotees!** *Fill in the blanks.*

Rāvaṇa	*Sugrīva*	*Bali*
Prahlāda	Mirabai	*Naciketas*
Draupadī	*Gajendra*	Narayana Bhattatiripad

1. Devotees who prayed in distress.

   ____
   ____
   ____

2. Devotees who sought limited ends in life.

   ____
   ____
   ____

3. Devotees who sought the Lord.

   ____
   ____
   ____

III. Find the different roles that one plays in daily life by filling in the missing letters.

1. __ __O__HE__

2. __R__ __N__

3. __TU__ __NT

4. __I__T__R

5. __ __V__T__E

6. __H__ __D

IV. Practise at home.

1. Create an altar for your favourite deity in your room and offer daily prayers at the altar. Tell why you chose the items you did and what they mean to you.

   ____

   ____

   ____

2. Among the many forms of worship, what is your favourite form? Learn to offer your daily prayers at home through practice of your favourite form of worship.

   ____

   ____

   ____

SURRENDER

'*Namaḥ*' is a very significant word, its meaning being what it is, in all religious traditions. In combination with the name of the Lord, its English translation is salutation or surrender unto the Lord. What is it that one surrenders or offers to the Lord?

In one's perception of oneself and the world, there are two orders of reality. One order is - it is there and therefore one sees it. Perceptually one hears a sound and inferentially concludes the source from which it comes. Both are verifiable, empirical facts. There is another reality which is - one sees therefore it is. One sees a blue sky but to conclude for want of knowledge, that there is a ceiling above the planet is false. Similarly, when one imagines something like a snake where there is only a rope, although there is a perception, it is erroneous. Though the fear that is invoked by the snake is empirically real, the order of reality of the cause of fear is purely subjective like that of dream - something exists because one sees it.

When a person thinks of the Lord, it is always with a concept that immediately creates a spatial distance between that Lord and oneself. By thinking of him as an entity with a given form, one keeps him remote from one's perception. This concept has developed from one's day to day experience. Seeing a pot one concludes there must be a potter because one does not see a natural source of pots in the world. All know that apples come from apple trees and gold from mines deep in the earth, but there is no such source for pots. Therefore, one concludes that there must be a potter who is an intelligent being capable of making pots. Without him or her, the pot cannot come into being of its own accord because it is inert. One presumes that there is an intelligent being other than oneself in this order of reality.

Extending this logic, one presumes that because there is a world in front, there must be a creator and because he is not seen on earth, he must be existing in a remote place in a certain form with particular attributes. This is very natural. And for prayer, it serves a purpose. But if questions are asked, this concept is not adequate.

And as long as these questions remain unanswered, one cannot put one's heart into any prayer. Children ask these basic questions and when they are not answered, they pray only to obey their parents and even if they continue to pray as adults, their heart is not in it. One must recognise that the human being is a rational person and if this fact is not respected, one is inviting trouble. In the native tradition of this land, this fact is totally respected.

Creation and the Creator

The logic behind the conclusion that just as there is a potter for the pot, there is a creator for the world, does not stand scrutiny. First, it has to be established that the pot as a created thing is comparable to the world. If there is a natural source from which pots spontaneously come into being, the creation of a pot is a valid model for the creation of the world. But there are no such natural pots. Therefore, along with the knowledge of the pot, is the knowledge that it has a creator. Similarly, when one sees a child, one immediately knows his/her parents exist. So, too, the appreciation of any creation reflects the immediate appreciation of the creator.

Can this logic be extended to the world? The fact that one sees it is not enough to prove it is a creation, like a pot. One knows the pot is made by a potter because one has seen a pot-maker making a pot, but one has never seen a world being made by a world-maker. And in order to assume that there is such an entity, this world must be an unnatural one. To conclude that this world is unnatural, one must see a natural world with reference to which this world is unnatural. Only then one can establish this world as a creation like a pot. Therefore, this line of thinking does not hold waters.

How then does one establish that this world is created? This is a creation because it is intelligently assembled. It is empirically true having an objective order of reality. It is, therefore I see. The body, mind, senses and the world are all intelligently put together. There must, therefore, be a creator who has the knowledge and power to create whatever is created. Any creation presupposes knowledge which always rests on a conscious being. In this creator of the entire creation, there must necessarily be all knowledge and all power. 'The entire creation', means everything that is known and unknown. In any given thing there is a known part and an even greater unknown part. Whatever one knows also includes a lot that one does not know. What is known and unknown constitute the entire creation. The creation must necessarily come from a conscious being and there are scriptural statements to support this such as 'that saw', 'he desired', 'he created'. This conscious being, the Lord is all-knowing, in general and in detail.

The Lord is the Maker and the Material

Anything that is created must also have a material. For example, unless the baker has something to bake, there is no loaf of bread. If the creator exists and is to create the world, he must have some material. Where does he find it? The question of 'where', is not appropriate because until the creation comes, there is no space. He can find the material for creation neither inside nor outside space because space is yet to come. Therefore, he can only find it in himself.

If the Lord is to create this world finding the material cause in himself, the Lord is both maker and the material. The model for this is one's own experience of sleep followed by dream. In sleep there is no time, no space, no world and no sense of individuality. And then one dreams. Time comes, space comes, everything that appears there comes from oneself. He/she is the creator of the entire dream world. There is no sequence in the things created, for instance, space is first created, then the sun, moon, earth and so on, are introduced one by one. All of it spontaneously arise at once. That one is capable of creation is true but what one has created is false; it is only subjective reality.

The world is put together. Its basic constituents are presented in the Veda as five elements - space, air, fire, water, earth - both subtle and gross. Every sense organ is born of a given subtle element. Any given body comprises space; air, in the form of oxygen and carbon dioxide; fire, because of which it maintains a particular temperature, water, which gives it shape; and the minerals and elements like calcium, carbon and so on. that are earth. The Vedic model of the universe is that it is a composite of these five elements intelligently put together. If it is understood that body is an assemblage of these five elements and the Lord is the creator and the material for all this, the whole universe is the Lord including one's body. The question - where is the Lord - is inappropriate as the Lord is the very space. Space being all pervasive, Lord is everywhere as everything.

What is it that one can surrender? One's dwelling place belongs to *Īśvara*, the very body belongs to *Īśvara*. All one can surrender is the notion 'they are mine'. No one owns anything; everyone is only a possessor. To claim ownership of something, one must be its sole author. Yet one finds oneself with a body, senses, the faculty to think, to explore, to remember and to know. These hands, legs, liver, kidney, the exterior world with all its bacteria and the capacity to deal with them, are all given. Truly, one does not own anything in all this, but one thinks he/she does and that causes a lot of problems. Once one says, "I am the owner of this", he is also saying, "I am not the owner of everything else". If one says, "I own this particular house on this street", implicit in that statement is "I do not own all the other houses". And if one owns the whole street, what about the rest of the city? Even if he owns the city what about other cities or the rest of the country? If he owns the whole country, what about the other continents, and even if he were to own the whole mother earth, what about the other planets, the whole system and other systems which one does not even know of. What one claims to own is miserably insignificant and what one does not own is vast.

Therefore when a person says '*namaḥ*' he is only asserting a fact and the individual is surrendered to the empirical, which is *Īśvara*.

✍ EXERCISE ✍

I. Fill up the blanks below:

1. __________________ creates pots with the material, ____________________.

2. Goldsmith creates __________________ from the material, ___________________.

3. __________________ creates __________________ from the material, yarn.

4. Carpenter makes __________________ from the material, ____________________.

5. __________________ bakes __________________ from the material, wheat flour.

6. __________________ builds the nest with the material, ____________________.

7. Shoe-maker makes __________________ from the material, ____________________.

8. __________________ makes ________________ from the material, herbs.

9. __________________ make __________________ out of earth.

10. ________________ sculpts a stone idol out of _________________.

II. Classify the following perceptions by placing them in the right basket.

Snake on a rope	Sunrise in the east	Ghost on a post
Dream world	Blueness of the sky	Mirage water
Twinkling stars	Blazing sun	Full moon
Sunset in the west	Castle seen in cloud formations	Silver on a shell

Basket A (subjective)*	Basket B (objective)**
____________________	____________________
____________________	____________________
____________________	____________________
____________________	____________________
____________________	____________________
____________________	____________________

*Perception is because you (alone) see.

** You see because it is there (seen by all).

III. Point to Ponder:

"Nobody really owns anything in the creation including one's body" - Discuss the truth of this statement by sharing with the class how everything is given to us by the Lord.

____

____

____

____

PRAYER

Prayer is the highest form of communication with the Lord and can be offered in simple words or as an elaborate ritual. The modes of prayer may differ from person to person, but the attitude is fundamental to all. Prayer helps nurture one's special relationship to the Lord - the relationship of the created to the creator - by invoking the devotee in the person. Unlike the other relative roles one plays, the role of a devotee is non-demanding since the Lord seeks nothing from us. When one's relationship to the Lord becomes primary in life, other relationships become secondary and thus less problematic.

Prayer is expressed in three ways: physical, *kāyika*; oral, *vācika*; and mental, *mānasa*. A ritual or a *pūjā* is a physical form of prayer. Singing in praise of the Lord or chanting verses and Vedic hymns is an oral prayer. *Japa* or worship done silently is mental prayer.

Prayer has its purpose in helping one achieve an object of desire, be it mental clarity or a given end. Ultimately, prayer helps one gain the maturity to be a qualified recipient of spiritual knowledge. This knowledge teaches us our identity with the Lord and helps us discover freedom and happiness, the nature of oneself.

In any pursuit, including education, there can be a number of obstacles, *tāpas*. These obstacles fall into three categories:

Ādhidaivika - Obstacles which are natural and over which we have no control, e.g., storms, earthquakes, floods.

Ādhibhautika - Obstacles created by one's surroundings, e.g., noisy neighbours, traffic, distractions by family.

Ādhyātmika - Obstacles created within oneself, e.g., tiredness, an agitated or distracted mind.

Any of these obstacles can prevent one from achieving success in a given endeavour. *Śānti*, peace is, therefore, chanted three times for the mitigation and the removal of these threefold obstacles.

The Purpose of Prayer

A prayer may carry a different intent for different individuals. In the *Bhagavad Gītā*, Lord *Kṛṣṇa* describes four types of devotees. The first one is called an *ārta*, a person in distress. He prays seeking relief from difficulties.

The second type of devotee is said to be the *arthārthī*, a person who seeks worldly ends. This is a person who is aware of the Lord's grace in his life, but whose motivation for prayer stems from seeking personal ends.

The third type of devotee is a *jijñāsu*, a seeker of knowledge. This person pursues knowledge for *mokṣa*, freedom from unhappiness. Though *mokṣa* is a desirable end for all, only a *jijñāsu* recognises knowledge as the means to this end and pursues it. His prayer is for inner growth and maturity, for the sake of gaining this knowledge.

The *jñānī*, a wise person is the fourth type of devotee. He knows his identity with the Lord. In the *Bhagavad Gītā*, Lord *Kṛṣṇa* describes the wise person as being one with the Lord. The *jñānī's* prayer is an expression of wisdom and is the highest form of prayer.

Prayer: Invoking the Unknown Factor

In order to accomplish any given end three factors are necessary. The first factor is adequate effort, *prayatna*. One cannot accomplish anything in life without adequate effort. The second factor is time, *kāla*. Once effort is made, time is necessary for the results to fructify. For example, when one sows a seed, time has to elapse for the plant to grow before it bears fruit. The length of time varies according to the nature of action and the result desired.

Despite making adequate effort and allowing sufficient time, the results may not always meet one's expectations. One's knowledge and power being limited, one cannot foresee and make things happen as one wants. There is always an unknown element, the third factor, often called chance or luck which a sensitive person understands as *daivam*, grace of the Lord. Such a person knows that the Lord's laws govern the results of actions and, through prayer, the person invokes the grace of those laws for obtaining desired results. The laws being non-separate from the Lord, prayer is efficacious in accomplishing any given end.

Like any other action, prayer produces a result. The result is twofold: one is immediately seen, *dṛṣṭaphala* and the other is unseen, *adṛṣṭaphala*.

The immediate result of prayer is the inner comfort that comes from acknowledging one's limited capacities and accepting a power higher than oneself. Being objective about situations over which one has no control and praying to that all-knowing source is an act that frees one from anxiety regarding the expectation of a result.

The unseen result of prayer refers to the subtle result called *puṇya*, which accrues to the doer of the action. *Puṇya* manifests in the form of comfortable situations whether in this life or later. When one prays for success, the accrued *puṇya*, which one may call 'grace', may not ensure success, but without it, the outcome could be worse.

Prayer is Always Answered

Prayer is always answered. When the Lord is omniscient, he knows better. Without prayers, things would have been worse. To illustrate this: Two boys were travelling. On the way they happened to see a *Gaṇeśa* temple. There is a Hindu custom that one should not pass a temple without offering salutations. So one of the boys went inside, while the other went ahead. The first boy, as he was returning after the worship, stepped on a scorpion on the temple door steps and got stung. He was shouting and screaming for help.

The second boy, as he was going, found on the road a gold coin. He came back to the first boy to inform him of the good luck. He saw the first boy seething with pain and came to know what had happened. He took this opportunity to ridicule his faith and told him that scorpion sting is the *prasāda* for devotion while golden coin is the reward for not going to the temple.

The first boy was already stung by scorpion and this thing stung him much more. He felt it was an injustice. He was not disinterested in the golden coin. He was a *bhakta* but at the same time was equally interested in money. Therefore he was very sad. Though he got help in the meanwhile and felt better, yet his mind was restless without an answer for the ridicule he got.

Later both the boys met a *sādhu* on their way. The *sādhu* happened to be an astrologer. He asked the dates and time of birth of both the boys. He calculated everything and told the boys all about their past. Having earned their appreciation, he said to the first boy that he should have been bitten by a cobra or have had an accident and he got away with a scorpion sting. To the other boy he said that he should have got a treasure but he had to settle for just a golden coin due to the lack of *puruṣārtha* in the form of prayer.

How the Prayer is Answered

Prayer is *puruṣārtha*. When a person prays it is of one's volition. Because of that *puruṣārtha*, the person neutralises or avoids greater pain. One always has some *prārabdha* coupled with *puruṣārtha*. Sometimes the *prārabdha* is against a person. Before doing any act one generally prays in order to neutralise *durita*, a bad part of his/her *prārabdha-karma* that brings problems to oneself. Day-to-day it brings problems. Morning is not like evening. In the evening everything is all right and suddenly one happens to fall down. A simple fall occurs and the person is in the hospital for three months. So this *durita* can be neutralised by *puruṣārtha* of prayer. Prayer does neutralise it. One does not know what one's *durita* was, how much of it was there. One who seems to have lost may be a gainer and vice versa. *Karmas* work in unknown ways and since prayer is a *puruṣārtha*, it has results.

One has to see the beauty of prayer. There is no meditation, no ritual, no act, without prayer because in any technique the will is retained. Here, the will willingly submits. That submission performs the miracle.

In this submission, human free will finds its total expression. This is so because one prays to the Lord who is invisible to the available means of perception and who is invoked in an inert object. That a person can offer salutation and prayers to an entity who is invisible takes the expression of the whole free will.

Prayer is thus centred on the person, the total person, and it comes from the person who sees very clearly his or her helplessness in a given situation. The situation is not centred on my will or even on my understanding. I give myself up not to despair, but into the hands of the Lord. The whole person that is me submits to the Lord. This is the meaning of surrender in prayer.

EXERCISE

I. Fill up the groups of two, three and four:

1. The result of prayer is two-fold:

   a) ______________ b) ______________

2. Prayer is expressed in three ways:

   a) ______________ b) ______________ c) ______________

3. Obstacles fall into three categories:

   a) ______________ b) ______________ c) ______________

4. In order to accomplish any given end three factors are required:

   a) ______________ b) ______________ c) ______________

5. Devotees are of four types:

   a) ___________ b) ___________ c) ___________ d) ___________

6. *Puruṣārtha*, human pursuits are four in number:

   a) ___________ b) ___________ c) ___________ d) ___________

II. Choose the right answer.

1. Prayer is
   a) a method of sitting
   b) an object of taste
   c) communicating with the Lord

2. The most exalted result of prayer is
   a) gaining true knowledge about oneself
   b) getting Rs.1,00,000/-
   c) destroying one's enemy

3. Prayer has
   a) no result at all
   b) only seen result
   c) both seen and unseen result

4. In a human being's life there are
   a) no obstacles at all
   b) only those obstacles that the individual himself wards off
   c) obstacles which cannot be removed without help from the Lord

III. Points to Ponder:

1. Prayers are always answered. But when I do not get what I want even after prayers, does my understanding of the above statement change?

   ____

   ____

2. I seem to gain what I want even when I do not pray. Then why should I pray in order to achieve what I want?

   ____

   ____

LORD APPRECIATED THROUGH *UPĀSANĀS*

The Sanskrit word '*upāsanā*' derives from the verbal root '*ās*' meaning 'to sit', combined with the prefix '*upa*' meaning 'near'. The literal meaning of *upāsanā* is, therefore, 'to sit near' or 'to think of the Lord'.

Upāsanā is generally translated as worship or meditation. When the worship is done exclusively in the mind, it refers to meditation. In the sense of meditation, *upāsanā* can be defined as "*saguṇa-brahma-viṣaya-mānasa-vyāpāraḥ*" - a mental activity whose object is the Lord. This mental activity can be in the form of *japa*, mental *pūjā*, or any other thought process centred on the Lord.

For meditation one requires an *ālambana*, a support, in the form of a symbol. When the symbol used is a form, the meditation is known as *pratimā-upāsanā*. When the symbol used is a name, the meditation is known as *pratīka-upāsanā*.

Pratimā Upāsanā

In Sanskrit, *pratimā-upāsanā* is defined as "*nikṛṣṭa-vastuni utkṛṣṭa-vastu-āropaḥ*" - superimposition of a superior object on an inferior one. For instance, Lord *Viṣṇu* is superimposed on a *śāligrāma*, a type of stone and then meditated upon. The inferior object can either be an icon, such as the image of a deity; or a non-icon, such as a *śāligrāma* representing Lord *Viṣṇu*; a *liṅga* representing Lord *Śiva*; a *kalaśa*, pot of water representing Lord *Varuṇa* or a *yantra* representing *Śrī Devī*.

Sometimes an object or a phenomenon with a particular characteristic is also chosen as a symbol of the Lord. For instance, when the sun is meditated on as *Brahman*, the ultimate reality, the sun stands for the light which symbolises omniscience.

Ascribing a higher significance to an ordinary object is not uncommon. For example, an ordinary piece of cloth of a particular form and colour can represent a nation and its ideals. Even though no one salutes a piece of cloth, saluting one's national flag is an expression of one's salutation and loyalty to one's country.

Pratīka Upāsanā

Meditation on a sound symbol such as the name of a deity, a *mantra*, a syllable, or a Vedic utterance is known as *pratīka-upāsanā*. The *Upaniṣads* describe *vyāhṛti-upāsanā* and *oṃkāra-upāsanā* as examples of meditation on sound symbols.

Some of the other forms of *upāsanās* are *śrī-cakra-upāsanā* and *ahaṃgraha-upāsanā*. In *śrī-cakra-upāsanā*, *Śrī Devī* is superimposed on a tantric symbol, which is made of lines arranged in a particular geometric pattern; while in *ahaṃgraha-upāsanā*, one meditates upon oneself as *Brahman*.

Various forms of *upāsanās* are given by the scriptures to help one attain a tranquil mind and an appreciation of the Lord. The *upāsanās* are based on the Vedic vision that the Lord is non-separate from the creation and therefore can be invoked in any given name or form. Until one appreciates this Vedic vision, one practices various *upāsanās* for gaining the inner disposition that will eventually lead one to the discovery of the Lord.

✍ EXERCISE ✍

I. Fill in the blanks with the words below to complete each sentence.

Om	*upāsanā*	*pūjā*	*pratimā*
pratīka	*dhyāna*	*śāligrāma*	*upavāsas*

1. A sound symbol is called __________________.

2. The Sanskrit word for meditation is __________________.

3. ________________ helps one gain a relatively tranquil mind.

4. In any ________________, one invokes the Lord in the form of a deity or an object.

5. ________________ is the name for *Brahman.*

II. True or False. *Check one.*

1. Superimposition of a superior object upon an inferior one is called *upāsanā*. T F

2. *Ahaṃgraha-upāsanā* is also called contemplation. T F

3. It is an uncommon phenomenon to ascribe a higher meaning to an ordinary object. T F

4. There are very few types of *upāsanās* described in the scriptures. T F

5. Respect shown to a country's flag is an example of *upāsanā*. T F

III. Answer these questions:

1. What is the purpose of meditation?

____

____

____

____

2. Give three examples where a higher meaning is ascribed to an ordinary object.

____

____

____

____

THE MEANING OF OM

Om is a very beautiful single-syllable word. In the *Kaṭhopaniṣad*, Lord *Yama* tells his student *Naciketas*: "All the *Vedas* talk about that goal to know which people take to a life of study and discipline and I will tell you that briefly. It is *Om*". Thus *Om* is something desired by people who seek freedom in life.

Om is derived from the Sanskrit verbal root '*av*', meaning 'to protect'. It refers to the Lord who protects and sustains everything. In other words, it is the name of the Lord in its various meanings.

Linguistic Meaning

Om is used as a *pratīka*, a symbol, for everything in the universe - this entire universe - because *Om* sustains everything. The entire universe means not only the physical universe, but also the experience thereof. This is the meaning the *Vedas* load in this symbol.

Being an oral tradition, *Vedas* explain *Om* as made up of three parts. These are phonetic parts of the sound '*Om*' and each of these parts are loaded with a certain meaning. That is called superimposition. You superimpose a meaning upon those sounds.

In *Om*, there are three letters '*a*', '*u*' and '*m*', the first two being vowels and the third, a consonant. Together these three letters form *Om*. The vowels '*a*' plus '*u*' becomes '*o*', a diphthong. The '*a*' and '*u*' are pronounced at the place of throat and lips respectively and the sound '*o*' arises from a combination of these two places. With the sound '*m*' at the end, it becomes *Om*.

The vowel '*a*' stands for the entire physical world of experience. The experiencer, the experienced and the experience, all the three of them, are covered by the sound '*a*'. When one is awake, one is aware of the physical body and the physical world - known and unknown. One is also aware of the experience of the physical world. At the same time, one is aware of oneself, the experiencer.

The vowel '*u*' stands for the thought world which is distinctly experienced as other than the physical world. When one dreams, imagines, or thinks, one experiences the thought world. The thought world, the object of that world and the experience of it are the meaning of the sound '*u*'.

The final sound '*m*' stands for the experience one has in deep sleep, the unmanifest condition. What was there before the creation and after the dissolution is the meaning of the sound '*m*'.

Thus, the sleeper and the sleep experience, the dreamer and the dream experience and the waker and the waking experience, all the three constitute 'everything' that is here. All these three together represent '*Om*'. *Om* is complete. This *Om* is a comprehensive name for the Lord and *Om* is the Lord.

As one chants *Om* repeatedly, the silence between the chants (called *amātrā*) stands for the awareness, the consciousness which is the basis of the three worlds, the three experiencers and the three states of experience. *Om* thus represents all that exists and the basis or substratum of all that exists.

Nonlinguistic Meaning of Om

The whole *jagat*, the manifest world, is seen as one, but severally, it has many forms. Each of these is seen as one thing and at the same time, it is a combination of several things. Even this physical body is one, but severally it has various parts. It consists of a face, a stomach, two hands, two legs and so on. Each part has many cells. The cells are of many types: liver cells, brain cells and so on. Each cell has many components like DNA, RNA and so on. Thus each object has a form for which a name is given. One keeps getting new words because there are different forms within each form. Thus the names and forms in the creation are endless.

All names and forms are not separate from the Lord. Now if one wants to give a name to the Lord in order to relate with him or communicate with him, what name should one give? One has to find a name that includes all names/forms. The word 'pot' does not include 'chair', or 'table', or 'tree', or 'carpet'. Nor does it cover any other word. Pot is only pot. The Lord is the one who is pot, chair, table, tree, carpet... everything. So if one has to name the Lord, one will have to recite the whole dictionary to cover all the names. And that is also not enough. One will have to do it in every language and every dialect of each language. And there are a lot of objects in the world which are yet to be known and one keeps on inventing new facts for which one discovers new names.

Thus, linguistically giving a name to the Lord - who is all names and forms is an impossible task. Therefore, one gives up language. In another explanation of *Om* which is non- linguistic, one does not look upon *Om* as a word, but sees it as phonetic.

All names are nothing but words. All words are nothing but letters and all letters are nothing but sounds. Letters or alphabets differ in each language. In English, alphabets are from A to Z. In Latin, alphabet starts with Alpha and ends with Omega. In Sanskrit, it goes from '*a*' to '*h*'. Thus letters are unique to each language. So one has to go beyond letters. All the individualities of languages are crossed here.

Beyond letters, a name becomes a group of sounds. The French, the Arab, the African tribesman, a Sanskrit scholar or a Boston Brahmin, all use sounds in communication. Especially when one does not know a language, one hears only sounds. In every language, certain sounds repeat themselves which are unique to that language.

Now if a Frenchman or an Indian or anybody else opens his mouth to make a sound, the sound that is produced is '*a*'. If one closes one's mouth and makes a sound, then the sound that is produced is '*m*'. No other sound is produced thereafter. And all the other sounds are in between '*a*' and '*m*' sounds, whether they are consonants or vowels.

Therefore, one sound that can represent all the other sounds is '*o*'. If one rounds one's lips and makes a sound, to round off all the sounds, in a sense, it will be '*o*'. The combination of all the three sounds is *Om*, which represent all the sounds. Hence *Om* is the best name of the Lord. When one utters *Om*, one has said everything.

Philosophical Meaning

The 'order' in the creation which is the basis for the existence of things and beings in the universe is non-separate from the Lord and *Om*, being the name of the Lord, this order is, therefore, *Om*. *Om* pervades everything in the world. How?

When we mention the order behind everything, it is not in terms of location. It is the very thing as such. For instance, when one analyses what makes a given cup, many questions arise. What is the material of the cup? Why can not mercury make a cup? Why does a cup appear in a given form? Why does it not have any other form? Why does it not rust, if it is a stainless steel cup? Why does the other cup, made of pig iron rust? It is all an order. A steel cup is a steel cup whenever one perceives it. If it loses its form tomorrow, that also is within the order. The flower that is seen today is gone tomorrow and there is a fruit - this is also within the order.

All the possibilities in the creation form part of the order. It is the order that makes a thing what it is. That a chair is a chair, is because of the order. Anything that is here is pervaded by this order. One is not going to get behind the objects to find the order. Order means how things are as they are. Every created thing is maintained by the order, called *niyati*. That *niyati* is *Īśvara*, the Lord, and *Om* being the name of the Lord, is the order behind the creation.

The scriptural teaching helps one to see this meaning of *Om* and connect it to the word '*Om*'. A word and an object denoted by the word, are one and the same. When one asks another to bring a pot, the other does not write 'p.o.t' and bring it. A word and the object meant by the word, are identical, in the sense that one cannot think of the word without thinking of the meaning. If one does not know the meaning then it is not a word - it only becomes a group of sounds. Once it is known that for this group of sounds this is the meaning, then without thinking of the meaning, one cannot think of the word. Thus, *Om* is a name of the Lord and being identical with the Lord, what it means is the truth of the Lord.

Oṃkāra as a Prayer

Om, as a sound symbol, indicates auspiciousness and is chanted at the beginning of prayers and Vedic studies. When one chants *Om* with the understanding that it is a name for the Lord, one can call him, invoke him or pray to him through *Om*. Hence many of the prayers, chants or *mantras* begin with '*Om*' and *Om* thus becomes a prayer for one's protection.

EXERCISE

I. Choose the correct answer.

Naciketas	*'a'*	*Liṅga*	*Yama*	*Śiva*
Om	*'m'*	*'a'*	*Om*	*'u'*

1. Identify the teacher and the student in *Kaṭhopaniṣad.*
   ______________________________ and ______________________________

2. Identify the *pratīka* and the *pratimā.*______________________ and
   ____

3. Identify the first sound and last sound in any language.
   ______________________________ and ______________________________

4. Identify the phonetic name and the linguistic name of the Lord.
   ______________________________ and ______________________________

5. Identify the letters which represent the dreamer and the waker in the linguistic analysis of *Om.*
   ______________________________ and ______________________________

II. Discover the Sanskrit Words. *Help yourself from the random meanings given below:*

silence Lord symbol the manifest world order

1. *a t m ā r ā*
2. *k r t a ī a p*
3. *g j a t a*
4. *y n a i i t*
5. *a ś ī v a r*

III. Points to Ponder:

1. Sounds can instantly bring to one's mind the object connected to the sound just as the mewing sound connects one to a cat. If you can see the phonetic meaning of *Om* very clearly, why should your mind not be immediately taken to the Lord on uttering or hearing the sound *Om*.

____

____

____

2. Combine any two Sanskrit vowels to form conjunct vowels and note how it helps you to pronounce the joining vowels easily. For example, 'a' + 'u' join to become 'o'.

____

____

____

Religious Disciplines

INTRODUCTION TO RELIGIOUS DISCIPLINE

As a child, one's actions are mainly impelled by one's needs. As one grows, however, one's actions are also guided by one's likes and dislikes. One gathers likes and dislikes from one's parents, from the surrounding environment, and also from the culture in which one grows up.

These likes and dislikes which form the basis of one's personality are twofold: binding and nonbinding. The likes and dislikes that make one dependent on situations are considered binding in nature. They are subjective and keep changing. One can be freed from the hold of binding likes and dislikes if one lives a life in keeping with *dharma*. Observance of religious disciplines helps one relatively neutralise likes and dislikes and develop strong will power.

Undertaking any discipline involves diligence, perseverance and single-pointedness in one's pursuit. When a discipline is backed by an appreciation of the Lord, it is considered a religious discipline. Such disciplines help bring about an awareness of the Lord's grace in one's life and a cheerful acceptance of all situations in life.

VOWS

A human being has the faculty of choice and can choose various courses of action. As the choices available to a person are many and varied, one often finds oneself confused in making choices. When a choice is made in keeping with universal values, one discovers a capacity to stand by one's resolve. Having the capacity to be firm in one's thinking and resolve is an asset and a mark of maturity.

A *vrata*, vow, is a form of self-discipline that one observes as a means for inner growth, thereby helping one develop a strong character. For example, one who makes a vow to be truthful in speech is called a *satyavrata*, one for whom truthfulness is a *vrata*. A wife who chooses the welfare of her husband as a vow and directs all her actions to that end is called *pativratā*, one for whom the husband is the object of the *vrata*.

In the *Bhagavad Gītā* (9.25) Lord *Kṛṣṇa* tells *Arjuna* that a vow made towards any given end helps an individual gain that end. Lord *Kṛṣṇa* says that those for whom the gods are the object of *vrata* reach the gods, and those for whom the ancestors are the object of the *vrata* reach the ancestors. The word 'reaching' in this verse does not mean 'going' in the literal sense, but refers to gaining a given end blessed by the gods or ancestors.

While some *vratas* are mandated by the *Vedas* in the form of injunctions, others are described in the *dharma-śāstra* and the *Purāṇas*.

Some of the *vratas* enjoined by the *Vedas* are:

1) *Savitra-vrata* - *vrata* taken for a period of time before one is initiated into the *Gāyatrī-mantra* at the time of *upanayana*.

2) *Brahmacarya-vrata* - a vow of celibacy during the period of Vedic study.

3) *Aupaniṣada-vrata* - *vratas* undertaken prior to the study of the various *Upaniṣads*.

4) *Snātaka-vrata* - *vrata* observed by one who has completed the scriptural study and is ready to enter the life of a householder.

The *dharma-śāstra* and the *Purāṇas* also prescribe several *vratas*. These are dedicated to the worship of various deities and are performed on specific days of the year. The days are chosen based upon astrological configurations and various stories in the *Purāṇas*. The *Purāṇas* tell stories of people who performed these *vratas* and how they benefited from them.

The different types of *vratas* that are widely practised are:

1) *Pūjā-vrata* - special *pūjās* to certain deities, such as *Śivarātri-vrata*, *Pradoṣa-vrata*, *Satyanārāyaṇa-vrata* and *Varalakṣmī-vrata*.

2) *Yātrā-vrata* - a vow to undertake a pilgrimage to a sacred place, *tīrtha*.

3) *Upavāsa-vrata* - fasting as a religious discipline. Fasting may be a *vrata* by itself or it may be a part of a *pūjā-vrata*.

4) *Japa-vrata* - chanting *mantras* in a specified manner, for example, *Gāyatrī-puraścaraṇa*.

5) *Mauna-vrata* - observing silence for a length of time.

6) *Prāyaścitta-vrata* - religious acts of atonement, such as taking a dip in a holy river.

7) *Pratijñā* - self-imposed resolve made by a person to observe a discipline, such as giving up a favourite food for a length of time.

In observing any religious discipline, it is important to use moderation, keeping in view the intent for which the action is undertaken. As Lord *Kṛṣṇa* points out in the *Bhagavad Gītā* (6.17), one should be moderate in one's actions.

युक्ताहारविहारस्य युक्तचेष्टस्य कर्मसु ।
युक्तस्वप्नावबोधस्य योगो भवति दुःखहा ॥

yuktāhāra vihārasya yuktaceṣṭasya karmasu
yuktasvapnāvabodhasya yogo bhavati duḥkhahā

yukta-āhāra-vihārasya - for one who is moderate in eating and other activities; *yukta-ceṣṭasya*- for one who is moderate in effort; *karmasu* - with reference to one's duties; *yukta-svapna-avabodhasya* - for one who is moderate in terms of sleeping and waking hours; *yogaḥ* - meditation (discipline); *bhavati* - becomes; *duḥkhahā* - the destroyer of sorrow

"For one who is moderate in eating and other activities, who is moderate in effort with reference to one's duties, and with reference to one's sleeping and waking hours, for such a person meditation (discipline) becomes the destroyer of sorrow."

EXERCISE

I. Circle the odd one out.

1. Disciplines observed by a person to develop a strong character are
   - a) fasting on special days
   - b) taking a pilgrimage
   - c) listening to music
   - d) observing silence for a length of time.

2. The purpose of undertaking a religious vow is
   - a) for one's inner growth
   - b) to diet
   - c) to atone for one's wrong actions
   - d) for self-discipline

3. A *vrata* is
   - a) a resolve that one makes to oneself
   - b) a part of the Vedic way of life
   - c) undertaken to gain direction in exercising one's freedom of choice
   - d) a revenge taken to destroy one's enemy

4. The *vratas* mandated by the *Vedas* are
   - a) *Brahmacarya-vrata*
   - b) *Aupaniṣada-vrata*
   - c) *Snātaka-vrata*
   - d) *Hiṃsā-vrata*

5. *Sītā*
   - a) is a *pativratā*
   - b) took *brahmacarya-vrata* for her entire life
   - c) is the wife of Lord *Rāma*
   - d) is King *Janaka*'s daughter

II. True or False. *Check one.*

1. In the *Gītā*, Lord *Kṛṣṇa* tells *Arjuna* that a vow made towards any given end helps an individual gain that end [T] [F]

2. The only vows one should follow are those mandated by the *Vedas*. [T] [F]

3. Likes and dislikes are objective. [T] [F]

4. Vows can be self-imposed. [T] [F]

5. In observing religious disciplines, it is important to be strict always. [T] [F]

6. A *Prāyaścitta-vrata* is a vow to visit a sacred place [T] [F]

7. The *dharma-śāstra* and the *purāṇas* describe vows dedicated to certain deities. [T] [F]

III. Name the different types of vows that are widely practised in the Vedic culture.

pūjā	*mauna*	*Prāyaścitta*	*pārāyaṇa*
yātrā	*japa*	*upavāsa*	*brahmacarya*

1. Special vows to certain deities are called ______________________ *vratas.*

2. A vow to undertake a pilgrimage is called a ______________________ *vrata.*

3. Fasting as a religious discipline is called an ______________________ *vrata.*

4. Chanting *mantras* in a specified manner is called ___________________ *vrata.*

5. Observing silence for a length of time is called ____________________ *vrata.*

6. Religious acts of atonement are called ______________________ *vratas.*

IV. Points to Ponder:

1. Have you seen anyone in your family observing a *vrata*? What was the purpose of this *vrata*?

2. Pick a *vrata* that appeals to you most and try to observe it on a holiday. Describe your experience.

WORSHIP

Pūjā is one of the most beautiful ways to bring out the devotee within oneself and establish a relationship with *Īśvara*, the Lord. *Pūjā* is called *kāyikaṃ karma*, an action involving one's limbs. It also includes speech and mental action in the form of chanting and thinking of the Lord.

In a physical form of worship, such as a *pūjā*, there is a greater field of expression of one's devotion than is possible in purely oral or mental forms of worship. The body, mind and speech are all involved in a *pūjā*. The forms, colours, fragrances and sounds of the various items of worship arrest one's mind and aid in evoking devotion in oneself.

A *pūjā* is performed in order to express one's gratitude to *Īśvara* for all one has been given in one's life. The very creation in which one is born is considered to be a gift of the Lord. The body-mind-sense complex is made up of five basic elements: space, air, fire, water and earth which also constitute the creation. Through the sense perceptions backed by the mind one perceives the Lord's vast creation and appreciates his glories.

Traditionally, a form of worship known as *pañcopacāra-pūjā*, worship with fivefold offering, is performed. This worship acknowledges the presence of the Lord and makes a simple offering of the five elements through a symbolic offering of *puṣpa*, flowers; *dhūpa*, incense; *dīpa*, light; *Naivedya*, food and *gandha*, sandalwood paste. These objects represent the elements space, air, fire, water and earth, respectively.*

Pūjā at Home

Pūjā is generally performed by an individual at home. Most homes have an altar where one or more deities are kept. The choice of deity is a personal one. It does not matter which deity is chosen as each one represents *Īśvara* in a different form or aspect. The deity that one chooses is called *Iṣṭa-devatā*, one's desired deity.**

Pañcāyatana Pūjā

Traditionally, those who strictly follow the Vedic way of life perform a *pūjā* called the *pañcāyatana-pūjā*. The following verse describes the deities worshipped in this *pūjā*:

आदित्यम् अम्बिकां विष्णुं गणनाथं महेश्वरम् ।
पञ्चयज्ञपरो नित्यं गृहस्थः पञ्च पूजयेत् ॥

ādityam ambikāṃ viṣṇuṃ gaṇanāthaṃ maheśvaram
pañcayajñaparo nityaṃ gṛhasthaḥ pañca pūjayet

ādityam - the sun deity; *ambikām* - Goddess *Ambikā*; *viṣṇum* - Lord *Viṣṇu*; *gaṇanātham* - Lord *Gaṇeśa*; *maheśvaram* - Lord *Śiva*; *pañca-yajña-paraḥ* - one committed to the five sacrifices; *nityam* - daily; *gṛhasthaḥ* - householder; *pañca* - five; *pūjayet* - may worship

"A householder who is committed to the performance of the *pañca-yajñas*, five daily sacrifices,*** may do *pañcāyatana-pūjā* daily to five deities: the sun deity, Goddess *Ambikā*, Lord *Viṣṇu*, Lord *Gaṇeśa* and Lord *Śiva*."

The five deities in this *pūjā* are traditionally invoked in the form of naturally occurring stones. For instance, *sphaṭika*, a crystal which occurs in various places in India, represents *Āditya* (the sun deity); stones with specific markings, obtained from River *Svarṇamukhī* in Andhra Pradesh, represents Goddess *Ambikā*; *śāligrāma*, obtained from River *Gaṇḍakī* in Nepal, represents Lord *Viṣṇu*; a red stone called *śoṇabhadra* from River *Śoṇā* represents Lord *Gaṇeśa*; and *bāṇa-liṅga*, obtained from River *Narmadā*, represents Lord *Śiva*.

The idols are placed in a prescribed manner. For *Śiva-pañcāyatana-pūjā* , Lord *Śiva* is placed in the centre, surrounded by the other deities; for *Viṣṇu-pañcāyatana-pūjā* , *Viṣṇu* is placed in the centre surrounded by the other deities and so on. For example, in *Śiva-pañcāyatana-pūjā*, the deities are placed as follows:

Ambikā		*Viṣṇu*
	Śiva	
Gaṇeśa		*Āditya*

A *pūjā* is performed to all the deities in either a five-step worship or a sixteen-step worship.

Steps of a *Pūjā*

Whether a *pūjā* is performed at home or in a temple, the essential steps are the same. The basic *pūjā* is called the *pañcopacāra-pūjā*, in which one makes a fivefold offering. A more elaborate *pūjā* is called the *ṣoḍaśopacāra-pūjā*, a sixteen-step *pūjā*, in which one additionally offers clothes, ornaments and other similar items that one enjoys. The most elaborate *pūjā* is called the *catuṣṣaṣṭi-upacāra-pūjā*, a sixty-four step *pūjā*, where the offerings include music, dance, chariots, elephants and other similar items. Whatever one enjoys in life can be offered to the Lord as an expression of gratitude.

With minor variations, the following steps are customarily followed in any *pūjā*. After taking a bath and preparing the altar, one sits in front of the altar in a comfortable posture. One begins the *pūjā* by lighting a lamp, which symbolises knowledge. In order to be prayerful, one invokes an attitude of purity within oneself by doing *ācamana*, which involves chanting the Lord's name three times and sipping water with each chant. This is followed by a prayer to Lord *Gaṇeśa*, who is the remover of all obstacles. Next, one performs *prāṇāyāma*, which helps one gain a relative composure of mind. *Saṅkalpa* is done next to identify the person, *yajamāna*, doing the *pūjā* , and to state the purpose for which the *pūjā* is done. Then one rings the bell. The sound of the bell is considered auspicious and is said to ward off negative influences from the place of worship.

Following these steps, one sanctifies water in the water pot through chants and purifies the various articles of worship by sprinkling the sanctified water on them. These articles include the place where one is seated, the bell and the flowers.

The *yajamāna* then offers prayers to the Lord within himself by reciting a verse in which one's body is likened to a temple and the self within is likened to the deity. As a final preparatory step one offers prayers to one's *Guru*.

The main *pūjā* may be brief or elaborate. It begins by invoking the presence of the Lord in a given symbol. This symbol may be a picture or an idol of a given deity, such as *Gaṇeśa* or *Lakṣmī*; or even a lump of turmeric powder; a betel nut; or a *kalaśa*, a brass pot of water. Once the Lord is invoked, the symbol is looked upon as the Lord until the *pūjā* is completed.

The Lord is treated as a revered guest. He is offered a regal seat and his feet are washed. He is then given a bath and offered clothes and various ornaments. Flowers are offered along with salutations. While offering flowers and salutations, the Lord is addressed by various names. They may be sixteen in number, one hundred and eight in number, or one thousand and eight in number. These names reveal the glories of the Lord and his essential nature. *Naivedya* is offered to the Lord in the form of freshly cooked food or fruits. The Lord is then provided with comforts and music and dance is offered unto him.

After the various offerings are completed, one offers *ārati* to the Lord by lighting a camphor and chanting prayers. Following the *ārati* one offers flowers and salutations. One concludes the worship by asking for forgiveness for any inadequacies, omissions and commissions in the performance of the *pūjā*. Once the *pūjā* is completed, the Lord is requested to return to his abode. The offerings that are made to the Lord are distributed as *prasāda* to everyone who participates in the *pūjā* .

Temple Worship

A temple is looked upon as the abode of the Lord. It is a place where people gather to offer worship to the Lord. There are thousands of temples in India, many of them magnificent and well known. There are many stories in the *Purāṇas* that explain how these temples became sacred and famous. The *sthala-Purāṇas* describe the various forms of worship associated with specific temples.

There are certain scriptural texts called *āgamas* which are the authority with regard to the different aspects of temple worship. There are three main *āgamas* connected to the worship of *Śiva*, *Viṣṇu* and *Śakti*. They describe in elaborate detail the selection of the site for a temple, temple construction, making of idols, installation of the deity and the consecration of the idols. They also describe the methods of worship, prayers and *mantras* associated with temple worship and the monthly and yearly festivals celebrated in a given temple.

The method of temple worship, while more elaborate, is essentially similar to the *pūjā* done at home. The temples in India have special features associated with them in regard to the form of worship offered by the devotees. The following are some examples:

Although the *Rāmanātha* Temple in *Rāmeśvaram*, Tamil Nadu, is located at the southern tip of India, the *śivaliṅga* at this temple is worshipped with water obtained from the *Gaṅgā*. At the Vadakkunathan Temple in Trichur, Kerala, *abhiṣeka* is performed to the *liṅga* with ghee.

At the Tirumalai Temple in Tirupati, Andhra Pradesh, offerings are made by dropping cash or jewels into a large hundi, collection box. Pilgrims shave their heads as an offering to the Lord. This symbolises giving up one's pride, as hair is looked upon as a symbol of vanity. Many pilgrims perform *aṅga-pradakṣiṇa*, circumambulating the temple by lying down and rolling, symbolising total surrender to the Lord.

At the *Kṛṣṇa* Temple in Guruvayur, Kerala, one recites *Nārāyaṇīya* composed by Narayana Bhattatiripad. At this temple, pilgrims make an offering called the *tulābhāra* in which one gives the Lord something valuable equal to one's weight. What is given generally depends upon the capacity and inclination of the pilgrim. It may be gold, silver, coconuts, bananas, grain, or any other object the person chooses.

The Palani Temple, in Tamil Nadu, is dedicated to Lord *Subrahmaṇya*. Pilgrims who visit this temple carry a kavadi upon their shoulders. This is an offering of food, milk and *pūjā* which has a puranic significance.

Even though worship is performed in many different ways, the ultimate goal for a devotee is dedicating all of his or her actions to the service of the Lord. Any action that one performs becomes a prayer to the Lord when done with an attitude of devotion and appreciation of the fact that nothing exists apart from *Īśvara*. It is this attitude, *bhāvanā*, that makes the life of a Hindu a religious life and a continuous process of spiritual growth.

* Refer to "Logic", Part 11.

** Refer to "*Iṣṭa Devatās*", Part 7.

*** Refer to "The Five Daily Sacrifices", Part 7.

EXERCISE

I. Categorise the items and deities that go with *Pañcāyatana Pūjā* and *Pañcopacāra Pūjā*.

Kṛṣṇa	*Āditya*	light	*Ambikā*
incense	food	*Viṣṇu*	flowers
Gaṇeśa	*Śiva*	cloth	sandalwood paste

PANCĀYATANA PŪJĀ	*PANCOPACĀRA PŪJĀ*
________________	________________
________________	________________
________________	________________
________________	________________
________________	________________

II. What is the unique form of offering at each of the following temples?

1. *Rāmeśvaram* Temple ________________
2. Tirupati Temple ________________
3. Vadakkunathan Temple ________________
4. Guruvayur Temple ________________
5. Palani Temple ________________

III. The various stones obtained from different rivers have associations with various deities. *Match the stone and deity.*

Viṣṇu	*Gaṇeśa*	*Ambikā*	*Śiva*
Āditya	*Subrahmaṇya*	*Lakṣmī*	

1. Stone with specific markings from *Svarṇamukhī* ______________.

2. *Śāligrāma* from *Gaṇḍakī* River ________________.

3. Crystal-like stone from various places in India ________________.

4. Red stone from *Śoṇā* River ________________.

5. *Bāṇaliṅga* from *Narmadā* River ________________.

IV. Field Work

1. Attend a *pūjā* at a nearby temple. Compare this *pūjā* with the *pūjā* done by a member of your family at home.

____

____

____

____

____

____

FASTING

Upavāsa is a vow which refers to fasting. The following verse explains the meaning of the word *upavāsa*:

उप समीपे यो वासः जीवात्मपरमात्मनोः।
उपवासः स विज्ञेयः न तु कायस्य शोषणम् ॥

upa samīpe yo vāsaḥ jīvātmaparamātmanoḥ
upavāsaḥ sa vijñeyaḥ na tu kāyasya śoṣaṇam

upa samīpe - *upa* meaning in proximity; *yaḥ* - which; *vāsaḥ* - abiding; *jīvātma-paramāt-manoḥ* - of individual and the Lord; *upavāsaḥ* - fasting; *saḥ* - that; *vijñeyaḥ* - is to be known; *na tu* - not; *kāyasya* - of the body; *śoṣaṇam* - emaciation

"May one know *upavāsa* as the abiding of the individual in proximity to the Lord and not merely the emaciation of the body."

One may misunderstand the goal of fasting to be the rigour of the physical discipline itself. This verse points out that the purpose of this discipline is not to starve the body but rather to gain a mature mind that can appreciate the Lord.

Deliberate fasting helps develop forbearance, *titikṣā*, which makes it easy for one to deal with the discomforts experienced in life. It is necessary to gain a certain degree of mastery in handling one's needs. One who does not have such a mastery can easily get frustrated and overwhelmed when one's needs are not met.

In *Āyur Veda*, an ancient system of medicine, fasting is described as being of benefit to one's physical health. It is said, "*laṅghanaṃ parama auṣadham*" - skipping a meal is the best medicine. Fasting provides the digestive organs with needed rest from their constant activity.

The *Bṛhadāraṇyaka Upaniṣad* (4.4.22) describes various disciplines meant for one's inner growth. One of these disciplines is called *anaśana*, which literally means not eating at all. *Ādi Śaṅkara* in his commentary on this *Upaniṣad* explains the meaning of *anaśana* as refraining from the obsessive enjoyment of sense pleasures, not as total abstinence from food. Thus, in observing a fast, it is important that one maintains moderation and does not emaciate one's body.

Since fasting is a religious vow, it is often undertaken at special times which are specified in the *dharma-śāstra*, such as *ekādaśī*.

Ekādaśī Fast

Ekādaśī is the eleventh day of the lunar cycle. It is a day when many Hindus fast. The *Padma Purāṇa* describes the importance of this day, the significance of the fast and the stories connected to it. *Ekādaśī* fasting is called *pūrṇa-upavāsa*, a complete fast, which means that one does not eat anything for twenty-four hours. The *dharma-śāstra* tells what one needs to do on this day in the following verse:

एकादश्यां तु कर्त्तव्यं सर्वेषां भोजन द्वयम् ।
शुद्धोपवासः प्रथमः सत्कथाश्रवणं ततः ॥

ekādaśyāṃ tu karttavyaṃ sarveṣāṃ bhojana dvayam
śuddhopavāsaḥ prathamaḥ satkathā-śravaṇaṃ tataḥ

ekādaśyām- on *ekādaśī*; *tu* - indeed; *karttavyam* - should be done; *sarveṣām*- by all; *bhojana* - O people; *dvayam* - two; *śuddha-upavāsaḥ* - complete fasting; *prathamaḥ* - first; *sat-kathā śravaṇam* - listening to the glories of the Lord; *tataḥ* - thereafter (the second)

"O people, these two things should be done on *ekādaśī* by all: first, complete fasting; and thereafter, listening to the glories of the Lord."

This discipline involves fasting and also spending time in prayer and in contemplation. According to the *dharma-śāstra*, the *ekādaśī* fast should be undertaken by one who is between the ages of eight years and eighty years of age and on the eleventh day of both the bright and the dark half of the lunar cycle. This fast has been highly praised and glorified in the puranic literature. The following verse says:

न गायत्र्याः परो मन्त्रः न मातुः परदैवतम् ।
न काश्याः परमं तीर्थं नैकादश्यास्समं व्रतम् ॥

na gāyatryāḥ paro mantraḥ na mātuḥ paradaivatam
na kāśyāḥ paramaṃ tīrthaṃ naikadaśyās samaṃ vratam

na - not; *gāyatryāḥ* - than *Gāyatrī*; *paraḥ* - greater; *mantraḥ* - *mantra*; *na* - not; *mātuḥ* - than mother; *paradaivatam* - greater god; *na* - not; *kāśyāḥ* - than *Kāśī*; *paramam* - greater; *tīrtham* - a place of pilgrimage; *na* - not; *ekadaśyāḥ* - of *ekādaśī*; *samam* - equal; *vratam* - vow (religious discipline)

"There is no *mantra* greater than *Gāyatrī*, no god greater than one's mother, no place of pilgrimage greater than *Kāśī* and no vow equal to *ekādaśī*."

The *Padma Purāṇa* cites the names of twenty-four *ekādaśīs* that occur in the year. One of the most famous is *Vaikuṇṭha-ekādaśī*, also known as *Mokṣa-ekādaśī*. It was on this day that Lord *Kṛṣṇa* taught the *Bhagavad Gītā* to *Arjuna*. This *ekādaśī* occurs in the month of *Mārgaśira* (November-December) and is dedicated to the worship of Lord *Viṣṇu*.

In *Viṣṇu* temples in South India, there is a door behind the sanctum called *Vaikuṇṭha-dvāra*, meaning the door to the heavenly abode of Lord *Viṣṇu*, which is opened only on this day. People pass through this door symbolically signifying their entry into *Vaikuṇṭha*.

Other Occasions for Fasting

Fasting during the day (sunrise to sunset) is undertaken on *caturthī*, the fourth day; *aṣṭamī*, the eighth day; and *caturdaśī*, the fourteenth day.

Many people in India fast on certain other days of the week also, like *soma-vāra*, Monday; *Maṅgala-vāra*, Tuesday; *Guru-vāra*, Thursday and *śani-vāra*, Saturday. These days of the week are dedicated to the worship of particular deities, for example, Monday for Lord *Śiva*; Tuesday for *Śrī Hanumān*; Thursday for *Guru*; Saturday for Lord *Viṣṇu* and Lord *Śani*.

One prescribed discipline involves fasting between sunset and sunrise. In observing this fast, one may refrain from all eating; one may avoid a staple food, such as rice or wheat; or one may eat only fruits. Such a fast is undertaken on *ravi-vāra*, Sunday; *amāvāsyā*, the new moon day; and *pūrṇimā*, the full moon day.

Another important occasion for fasting is during the solar and the lunar eclipses. One fasts for six hours before the actual eclipse occurs and ends the fast when the eclipse is over. One also spends that time in prayer and contemplation. On such occasions, large numbers of people also take a holy dip in the *Gaṅgā* near Haridvar, *Kāśī*, Prayag and *Kurukṣetra*.

Fasting is also undertaken as part of a *pūjā*. On such days one undertakes a fast until one completes the *pūjā*. Some of these occasions include *Śivarātri*, *Rāmanavamī* and *Satyanārāyaṇa-pūjā* day.

EXERCISE

I. Circle the correct answer.

1. Fasting on chosen days helps one

   a) develop inner strength
   b) earn money
   c) learn Sanskrit

2. *Ekādaśī* is

   a) the first day of the lunar cycle
   b) the eleventh day of the lunar cycle
   c) a day of feasting

3. On *Ekādaśī*, along with fasting, one must

   a) go to the movies
   b) spend time in prayers
   c) not do homework

4. The *Ekādaśī* fast has been glorified in the following words:

   a) Fasting on *Ekādaśī* leads to loss of appetite.
   b) Fasting on *Ekādaśī* helps improve one's memory.
   c) In efficacy there is no *vrata* equivalent to *Ekādaśī*.

5. In the *dharma-śāstra* it is said that fasting should be undertaken by one who is

   a) between the ages of eight years and eighty years
   b) desirous of wealth
   c) on his death bed

II. Fast or Feast! *Choose the days listed and fill in the blanks.*

Ekādaśī	*Dīpāvali*	Solar Eclipse Day
Śivarātri	*Vijayalakṣmī*	*Makara-saṅkrānti*

1. FASTING DAYS

   ____

   ____

   ____

2. FEASTING DAYS

   ____

   ____

   ____

III. Points to Ponder:

1. Name some of the days when people of other religions observe fasting. Discover similarities of their observances with Hindu fasting.

   ____

   ____

   ____

2. Have you ever successfully observed a religious fast? Share how you felt physically and mentally that day. Will you do it again? Why?

   ____

   ____

   ____

JAPA

Japa is an oral form of worship. It is also a mental activity which allows one to recognise the patterns of one's thinking and gain a tranquil mind. In order to understand how *japa* works one needs to understand how the mind functions.

The mind is a flow of thoughts. Even though the mind seems to have its own logic by which one thought leads to another, this is not a conscious process. No one knows what his next thought will be. Thus one seems to have no control over one's mind.

Japa as a Technique

Japa is a technique whereby one can appreciate the ways of the mind. In *japa* one repeatedly chants a *mantra*, a particular word or a brief sentence. The three forms of *japa* are *ucca-japa*, where one chants a name of the Lord or a *mantra* vocally and audibly; *manda-japa*, where one's chanting is vocal but not audible to others; and *citta-Japa*, where one's chanting is purely mental. This *japa* is also called *dhyāna*, meditation.

In *japa*, one gives the mind a specific function to perform. Since it involves chanting the same word or sentence repeatedly, thoughts are not allowed to form their loose connections. Other functions of the mind, such as memory and deliberation, are also avoided. Because the same chant or *mantra* is repeated, there is no memory involved as in chanting a lengthy prayer. If one simply repeats the *mantra* without paying attention to its meaning, the intellect also does not operate. In this manner one deliberately creates in one's mind a situation wherein the thoughts are predictable, and the various usual mental functions are minimised. Once the mind has been given this occupation, one is more readily aware of any thought that comes to the mind that is different from the *mantra*. One dismisses this thought and brings the attention back to chanting the *mantra*.

By this process one learns to be alert to one's thoughts as they arise, to dismiss unwanted thoughts and to retain thoughts that are conducive. Thus, one benefit of *japa* is an increased alertness in one's own thinking patterns and greater mastery of the mind.

Discerning the Self as Silence

A more significant purpose of *Japa* is discerning the nature of the self as silence. When one repeats a *mantra*, the usual connecting pattern between two thoughts is eliminated. The mind does not follow its usual connections, since the same thought keeps recurring. Each thought is a complete unit by itself, unconnected to the next or previous thought. Between two thoughts there is an interval, during which there is no particular thought. The interval between two thoughts has no particular form or shape and is what we call silence or tranquillity, *śānti*.

Generally, tranquillity is looked upon as a mental state to be acquired by doing something. In fact, one does not do anything to achieve the silence that is there between two thoughts. Thus, while doing *japa*, there is "thought, silence, thought, silence, thought, silence". Through the practice of *japa*, one comes to appreciate the silence between two thoughts.

When one recognises one's nature to be silence, then one understands that all thoughts arise in silence, exist in silence and resolve into silence alone. If one's nature were thoughts, then one would always be thinking, but this is not so. Thoughts are absent in deep sleep, as well as between two successive thoughts. This appreciation of the essential nature of oneself as being non-separate from silence does not take place by the process of *japa* alone. Such an understanding takes place by exposing oneself to the teaching of the scriptures. *Japa* creates a situation by which what is understood gains greater clarity.

Mental Prayer

If *Japa* were merely a mental technique, then any sound would be able to serve the function of a *mantra*. However, one cannot seriously sit and chant meaningless sounds. *Mantras* are meaningful words that have a sanctity due to their association with the Lord. When one does *japa* by chanting a *mantra*, one also invokes in oneself the relationship of a devotee to the Lord. Any relationship carries a relative role with it and implies certain limitations and conflicts. The relationship of the devotee to the Lord is a fundamental one as it is a relationship of the individual to the total. It is also a role that is relatively free of conflicts. Thus when one sits and does *japa* as a devotee, one immediately evokes in oneself a relatively composed mind, because the distractions attached to the usual relative roles are minimised. Being a word or a phrase whose meaning is connected with the Lord, the *mantra* is a mental prayer, making *japa* more than a mere technique.

There are certain traditional *mantras* that are chanted in *japa*. Two common *mantras* are "*oṃ namaḥ śivāya*" and "*oṃ namo nārāyaṇāya*". Traditionally one receives a *mantra* from one's *Guru*. The *Guru* selects a *mantra* based on his knowledge of the student, and gives the *mantra* a special sanctity. If this is not possible one can select a *mantra* on one's own and do *Japa*.

Use of the *Japa Mālā*

A *Japa-mālā* is very useful as an aid in the practice of *Japa*. A *Japa-mālā* is a garland of beads, similar to the rosary found in many religions, including Christianity, Islam and Buddhism. A *Japa-mālā* is made of 108 beads. One additional bead is attached to the *mālā* but is separate from the rest. This is called the *meru* bead.

The Sanskrit alphabet consists of fifty-four letters. Repeated forward and backward, the total is 108. As any name of the Lord, whether known or unknown, is included within these letters, the number 108 represents the Lord.

The *Japa-mālā* is held in one's right hand. The ring and the little fingers are held together with the *mālā* hanging upon the ring finger. A single bead is grasped by the thumb and the middle finger and moved towards the palm while chanting one *mantra*. This process continues until one reaches the *meru* bead. At that point, one turns the *mālā* around and continues chanting in the same way. This process is called telling the beads. Each bead represents one chant of the *mantra*. With a little practice one can easily learn how to use the *Japa-mālā*.

Using a *Japa-mālā* while chanting *mantra* is very helpful. The chanting of the *mantra* comes to be closely associated with telling the beads. When one gets distracted, or one unconsciously stops chanting the *mantra*, the movement of the *mālā* also stops. This is another means by which one is immediately made aware of one's distractions from the chanting.

In the *Bhagavad Gītā* (10.25) Lord *Kṛṣṇa* points out the importance of *japa* by saying, "*yajñānāṃ japa-yajño'smi*" - among the *yajñas*, rituals, I am *japa*. There are many forms of rituals by which the Lord is invoked. Here Lord *Kṛṣṇa* mentions *japa* as the best form of worship by identifying himself with *japa*.

The following verse also describes the glory of *japa*:

जकारो जन्मविच्छेदः पकारः पापनाशनः ।
जन्मकर्महरो यस्मात् तस्माज्जप इति स्मृतः ॥

jakāro janmavicchedaḥ pakāraḥ pāpanāśanaḥ
janmakarmaharo yasmāt tasmajjapa iti smṛtaḥ

jakāraḥ - the syllable '*ja*'; *janma-vicchedaḥ* - (is the) destroyer of the (cycles of) birth; *pakāraḥ* - the syllable '*pa*'; *pāpa-nāśanaḥ*- (destroyer) of all impurities; *janma-karma-haraḥ* - the destruction of cycles of birth (and death) and impurities; *yasmāt* - because; *tasmat*- therefore; *japaḥ* - *Japa*; *iti* - thus; *smṛtaḥ* - is called

"The syllable '*ja*' signifies the end of the cycle of birth. The syllable '*pa*' stands for the destruction of all impurities. Therefore that by which the cycle of birth (and death) and all impurities are destroyed is called *japa*."

Thus, *japa* serves as a prayer and as a useful technique for understanding the ways of the mind.

✍ EXERCISE ✍

I. Circle the odd one out.

1. *Japa* is
   a) a physical exercise
   b) repeated chanting of a word or sentence
   c) a mental activity
   d) a religious activity

2. In *japa*, one's chanting may be
   a) audible
   b) not audible
   c) mental
   d) none of the above

3. *Japa* is beneficial because it
   a) helps one gain an increased alertness to one's thinking patterns
   b) helps one forget the outside world
   c) helps one discern tranquility which is the nature of oneself
   d) is a mental prayer

4. Some of the *mantras* traditionally chanted are
   a) *oṃ hari*
   b) *oṃ namaḥ śivāya*
   c) *oṃ namo nārāyaṇāya*
   d) *oṃ namo bhagavate vāsudevāya*

5. A *japa-mālā*
   a) has one bead known as "*meru*"
   b) is a garland of beads
   c) is different from a rosary
   d) is generally made of 108 beads

II. Answer these questions:

1. On what religious day does one chant "*oṃ namaḥ śivāya*"?

____

____

2. What is the meaning of the word *japa*?

____

____

3. Where does Lord *Kṛṣṇa* say, "Among the rituals, I am *japa*"?

____

____

4. What does "telling the beads" mean?

____

____

5. What does 108 beads on a *japa-mālā* signify?

____

____

III. Practise at home.

In your *pūjā* room at home, spend ten minutes every day doing *japa*. Recite your favourite *mantra* by telling the beads 108 times. Observe your mental disposition before and after doing *japa*. Share your experience with the class.

____

____

SILENCE

Mauna is a religious discipline that involves refraining from speaking. This discipline helps one develop an introspective as well as a contemplative mind. The one who has such a mind is called a *muni*, a contemplative person.

Often speech is used as a means of escaping from oneself. People engage in many futile and meaningless conversations throughout the day. By doing so, they keep their minds occupied and avoid facing themselves. It is only when one stops speaking for a length of time that one tends to be more aware of one's thoughts. Instead of focusing one's attention on expressing oneself through speech all the time, during *mauna* one focuses one's attention on thinking. Practising *mauna* helps one gain an alertness in one's thinking and speech.

While observing *mauna* as a vow, one thinks of the Lord through various acts. One may engage oneself mentally with prayer, chanting verses and hymns, and doing *japa*, all of which help to connect oneself to the Lord. Refraining from speech should be total, in the sense that one avoids other forms of communication, such as writing and sign language.

The days that are prescribed for undertaking *mauna* are *soma-vāra*, Monday; *Guru-vāra*, Thursday; and *ekādaśī*, eleventh day of the lunar cycle. People who worship *Devī*, observe *mauna* on Fridays and during the festival of *Navarātri*.

There is a mandate in the *dharma-śāstra* that says, "*maunena bhoktavyam*" - may one eat in silence. This mandate is reflected in the common custom in India wherein people refrain from talking while eating. They look upon eating as a *yajña*, a worship, in which food is considered to be an offering to the Lord within oneself.

EXERCISE

I. True or False. *Check one.*

1. In the Vedic culture one is advised to refrain from talking while eating. [T] [F]
2. *Mauna* is a *vrata* that involves chatting with another person. [T] [F]
3. *Mauna* helps put one to sleep. [T] [F]
4. The discipline of *mauna* helps one observe and regulate what one thinks. [T] [F]
5. *Devī* worshippers observe *mauna* during the *Navarātri* festival. [T] [F]
6. Some ascetics practise *mauna* for twenty years. [T] [F]

II. Point to Ponder:

"Silence is Golden." - What does this saying mean to you?

____

____

____

III. Practise at home.

Try to observe silence for half-a-day. During this time observe the ways in which your mind thinks. Did you want to talk to others? How did you feel after not talking for a couple of hours?

____

____

____

RESOLVE

A *pratijñā* is a religious discipline which one makes in the form of a resolve or pledge, to the Lord or to another person. Making a pledge to the Lord may be connected with a desire to achieve something. For example, one may make a pledge that upon accomplishing something that one wants, one will give a certain amount of money to charity. In making such a pledge, one may have a selfish motive. However, there is also an acknowledgement of the Lord as being the giver of the results of one's actions. It is this recognition of the Lord that makes the pledge a religious discipline. Some individuals make a pledge of giving a certain portion of their income for charity in gratitude for what they have been given.

A pledge may be in connection with a given occasion or may continue for a lifetime. Traditionally a *pratijñā* is made when one visits *Vārāṇasī*. One pledges to give up a favourite vegetable or fruit for the rest of one's life. This helps one develop self-discipline by serving as a constant reminder of one's commitment to spiritual growth.

Other *pratijñās* include fasting for a given period of time and performing special *pūjās*, such as the *Sātyanārāyaṇa-pūjā* every year for a given number of years.

In the *Mahābhārata* there is a story of a great character named *Bhīṣma* who made a powerful resolve, known as the *Bhīṣma-pratijñā*. It is said that *Bhīṣma* took a vow of celibacy to enable *Satyavatī* to marry his father, King *Śantanu* and to ensure that their child would become heir to the throne of *Hastināpura*. *Bhīṣma* is admired for his perseverance and commitment to this vow. Even today, when a person makes a resolve and honours it, his commitment is referred to as a *Bhīṣma - pratijñā*, and that person commands respect in the society.What resolve one makes is one's own choice. What is important is living up to the pledge that one has made.

EXERCISE

I. Circle the correct answer.

1. A *pratijñā* is a vow one makes in the form of a
   a) speech
   b) song
   c) resolve

2. A *pratijñā* is made to
   a) the Lord or a person
   b) the Lord
   c) oneself

3. In making a *pratijñā* there is an acknowledgement that
   a) I want to accomplish something
   b) the Lord is the giver of the results of one's actions
   c) I have no will power

4. A great historical figure who is famous for a *pratijñā* he made to his father
   a) *Bhīṣma*
   b) *Śvetaketu*
   c) *Yudhiṣṭhira*

5. Customarily a *pratijñā* is made when one
   a) visits Kanyakumari
   b) goes to a temple
   c) makes a pilgrimage to *Vārāṇasī*

6. What is important in a *pratijñā* is that one
   a) lives up to the pledge that one has made
   b) gives away as much money as possible
   c) follows it at least for a short time

II. Match the persons with the vows each took. *Fill in the blanks with the words below to complete each sentence.*

Kṛṣṇa	*Bhīṣma*	*Bharata*
Karṇa	*Bhīma*	*Draupadī*

1. ________________ vowed to kill *Duryodhana.*

2. ________________ took a vow of celibacy.

3. ________________ pledged his friendship with *Duryodhana.*

4. ________________ vowed not to fight in the *Mahābhārata* war.

5. ________________ took a vow of self-immolation if *Rāma* failed to return to *Ayodhyā* at the end of the exile.

III. True or False. *Check one.*

1. A *pratijñā* strengthens one's will power. [T] [F]

2. A *pratijñā* is always mandated by the *dharma-śāstra* [T] [F] .

3. When one visits *Kāśī* one takes a vow to eat on *Ekādaśī* day. [T] [F]

4. *Bhīṣma* resolved to occupy the throne of *Hastināpura* at the death of King *Śantanu.* [T] [F]

5. A *pratijñā* may be made for a specific occasion, for a number of years, or for a lifetime. [T] [F]

IV. Points to Ponder:

1. Describe a *pratijñā* you made in your life. Were you successful in honouring your resolve?

____

____

____

2. Many people make New Year resolutions at the beginning of each year. List some common resolutions that people make and what their reasons may be for making them. Give few reasons why one may not successfully be able to fulfill such resolutions for the year. How can one gain the discipline to overcome these obstacles?

____

____

____

EXPIATORY RELIGIOUS VOWS

Prāyaścitta-vrata is an expiatory religious discipline undertaken as an atonement for one's wrong actions. It is believed that the results of wrong actions become the cause of one's sorrow and pain in life. While one cannot retract one's past actions, certain religious vows can be undertaken to neutralise their effect.

Some of the expiatory religious vows are observed through fasting.

Cāndrāyaṇam

One type of fast that is commonly practised in India is called *Cāndrāyaṇa*. It is a form of fasting in which the food intake is highly regulated. This discipline requires much effort and will power. During this period, specific rituals are also performed. Two types of *Cāndrāyaṇa* are well known.

The first type of fast begins on *pūrṇimā*, the full moon day and ends on the next *pūrṇimā*. On the full moon day one eats fifteen morsels of food. The intake of food is reduced by one morsel each day thereafter. One fasts on *amāvāsyā*, the new moon day, then starts eating one morsel and increasing food intake by one morsel each day, until the next full moon day.

The second type of fast begins on *prathamā*, the first day after *amāvāsyā*, the new moon day and ends on the next *amāvāsyā*. One begins by eating one morsel on the first day after the new moon day and increasing the food intake by a morsel a day, reaching fifteen morsels on the full moon day. Then one reduces the intake by one morsel a day ending in a full fast on the new moon day.

Other expiatory religious vows include undertaking a *yātrā*, pilgrimage; doing *Japa*, chants; performing *snāna*, purificatory bath; and performing special *karmas*, rituals, which include giving *dāna*, charity.

EXERCISE

I. True or False. *Check one.*

1. *Prāyaścitta-vrata* is an expiatory religious vow. T F

2. Religious vows do not require much effort and will power. T F

3. One undertakes certain religious vows in order to negate the effects of *pāpas* that have accrued to oneself. T F

4. Some of the *prāyaścitta-vratas* are in the form of making merry. T F

5. There are two types of *cāndrāyaṇa* fasts T F

II. Points to Ponder:

1. Name three *prāyaścitta-vratas* that one can undertake?

___

___

___

2. "One can make amends." What does this saying mean?

___

___

___

3. Is apologising to someone a form of *prāyaścitta*? Explain.

___

___

___

PILGRIMAGE

In India, there are many places of worship which have gained sanctity over the centuries. There are stories in the *purāṇas* associated with different places where devotees felt the presence of the Lord.

It is one's attitude, called *bhāvanā* in Sanskrit, that makes a place sacred. It is only when one visits a place of worship with an attitude of devotion that one will be blessed. A person who visits the same place as a tourist, without an attitude of devotion, will not be blessed.

In the fourth *skandha* of the *Devī Bhāgavata*, Sage *Ajāvana* glorifies the attitude of devotion. He tells *Prahlāda* that even though many people live on the banks of the sacred river *Gaṅgā* and bathe in its holy waters, they do not benefit from it without an attitude of devotion. In the *Padma Purāṇa* it is stated that it is one's devotion and the purity of one's mind that blesses one who visits sacred places. It is because of this attitude that one is designated as a pilgrim and his journey to the temple is called a *yātrā*, pilgrimage. There are certain pilgrimages that are considered important in the life of a Hindu. Some of them are as follows:

Tristhalī Yātrā (Pilgrimage to Three Places)

It is believed that every person owes three debts in his life. The first debt is to the gods for what one is blessed with; the second debt is to one's forefathers who have left the legacy of culture and knowledge; and the third debt is what one owes to oneself for one's spiritual growth. One fulfills these debts by making a pilgrimage to Prayag, *Kāśī* and *Gayā*.

The *tristhalī-yātrā* has been extolled in many *Purāṇas*, such as *Padma Purāṇa*, *Vāyu Purāṇa*, and *Matsya Purāṇa*.

There are certain customs that are traditionally followed in making the *tristhalī-yātrā*. One first goes to *Rāmeśvaram* where *Śrī Rāma* is supposed to have performed *pūjā* to Lord *Śiva*. One worships Lord *Śiva* by making three *liṅgas* with sand. One *liṅga* is carried to Prayag where it is immersed in the waters of the *Triveṇī* (*Gaṅgā*) after one performs worship and takes a holy bath in the river. By doing this, one fulfills the debt to oneself.

One then goes to *Kāśī* where one takes a holy dip in the waters of the *Gaṅgā* and worships Lord *Śiva* fulfilling one's debt to the various deities. From here one goes to *Gayā* where one makes offering of rice balls, *piṇḍas*, to one's forefathers, at three places. One place is on the banks of the River *Phālguna* and the offering made here is called *tīrtha-śrāddha*. The second offering is performed at a site called *Viṣṇu-pāda* and the third is at a place called *vaṭa-vṛkṣa*. The third offering is called *akṣaya-vaṭa-śrāddha*. By doing this, one fulfills the debt to one's ancestors.

After visiting *Gayā*, one returns to Prayag and takes a dip in the *Gaṅgā*. Taking *Gaṅgā* water, one returns to *Rāmeśvaram* and performs *abhiṣeka* to the *śivaliṅga*. Those who live in North India go to *Kāśī*, *Gayā* and Prayag, from where they take *Gaṅgā* water to *Rāmeśvaram* and bring back the sand to Prayag to immerse it in the *Gaṅgā*.

Sabarimalai *Yātrā*

This pilgrimage is generally undertaken by men. It is preceded by a *vrata*, a deciplined life for one *maṇḍala* (forty days). During this time, a man lives a life of celibacy and strict vegetarianism, wears black or blue clothes; and performs special prayers. To reach the temple which is situated on a hill he treks through a forest route for two days. On the journey he carries two bags called irumudikattu, one containing a coconut filled with ghee and other items for worship and the other containing items for his own travel. The pilgrimage culminates when he reaches the temple of Lord Ayyappa at Sabarimalai on *Makara-saṅkrānti* day.

Chardham *Yātrā*

This is a pilgrimage to four sacred places, collectively called Chardham, located in the Himalayan range. They are Gangotri, where the River *Gaṅgā* originates; Yamunotri, where the river *Yamunā* begins her journey; Badrinath, where there is a temple dedicated to Lord *Viṣṇu*; and Kedarnath, one of the *jyotirliṅga-kṣetras.** This pilgrimage is undertaken between the months of May and October, as these places are inaccessible in winter months.

Amarnath *Yātrā*

Amarnath is situated in the eastern recesses of Kashmir. The shrine is reached by a hard and strenuous trek for thirty miles from a place called Pahalgam in Kashmir. The round trip journey is accomplished in six parts in six days. Devotees reach the cave of Amarnath on the *Śrāvaṇa-pūrṇimā* day and worship Lord *Śiva* in the form of a snow *liṅga*.

Lord *Subrahmaṇya* Temple *Yātrā*

An ancient Tamil work written by the great poet Nakkirar over two thousand years ago describes the glories of the six abodes of Lord *Subrahmaṇya*. People undertake a pilgrimage to visit these six abodes located in Tamil Nadu seeking refuge from physical ailments. They are Thirucchendur, Palani, Svamimalai, Thirupparankundram, Palamudirsolai and Thiruttani.

* Refer to "Places of Pilgrimage", Part 8.

EXERCISE

I. Fill in the blanks with the words below to complete each sentence.

tīrtha	forty	fourteen
devotion	*Gayā*	*Rāmeśvaram*

1. A pilgrimage does not benefit a person unless he or she has an attitude of _________________.
2. The Sanskrit word for a pilgrimage centre is _________________.
3. *Tristhalī-yātrā* covers three *tīrthas*: *Kāśī*, Prayag and _________________.
4. In making a *yātrā* to Sabarimalai, devotees observe *vrata* for _________________ days.
5. The offering of *Gaṅgā* water to Lord *Śiva* at _________________ is considered to be meritorious.

II. Field Work

1. Going on a *yātrā*, pilgrimage, often includes taking relevant vows. Find out what types of pilgrimages and vows are undertaken by people belonging to different religions and see how they compare with the Hindu *yātrā*.

____

____

2. Have any of your relatives been on a pilgrimage? Find out and share their *yātrā* experiences with the class.

____

____

THE FIVE DAILY SACRIFICES

To live in harmony with the world one needs to recognise one's place within the larger scheme of things. One also needs to be sensitive to oneself, to others and to the environment. One sign of emotional maturity is the ability to interact with others gracefully and to deal effectively with whatever situations one encounters.

One who is sensitive and mature does not take anything in the creation for granted. Such a person is grateful to the Lord for all that he has been given in life. To express one's appreciation one performs the five daily acts of worship called *pañca-yajñas.* These are enjoined in the *Taittirīya Āraṇyaka* section of *Kṛṣṇa Yajur Veda* (*mantra* 2.10.1). The *Manu Smṛti* (3.70) identifies these fivefold sacrifices in the following verse:

अध्यापनं ब्रह्मयज्ञः पितृयज्ञस्तु तर्पणम् ।
होमो दैवो बलिर्भौतो नृयज्ञोऽतिथिपूजनम् ॥

adhyāpaṇaṃ brahmayajñaḥ pitṛyajñastu tarpaṇam
homo daiva balirbhauto nṛyajño'tithi pūjanam

adhyāpaṇam - teaching; *brahma-yajñaḥ* - the act of worship to the *Vedas*; *pitṛ-yajñaḥ* - the act of worship to ancestors; *tu* - whereas; *tarpaṇam* - offering of oblations of water, rice and sesame seeds to ancestors; *homaḥ* - fire ritual; *daivaḥ* - (sacrifice) to gods; *Baliḥ* - giving food; *bhautaḥ* - (sacrifice) to living creatures; *nṛ-yajñaḥ* - sacrifice to human beings; *atithi-pūjanam* - service to guests

"The ritual to the *Vedas* is in the form of teaching the *Vedas*; the ritual to ancestors is *tarpaṇa*; the ritual to gods is the fire ritual; the ritual to living creatures is giving food; and the ritual to human beings is service to guests."

Brahma Yajña

Brahma here means the *Vedas*. Every *vaidika* has the duty to study the *Vedas* daily, based on the scriptural injunction, "*svādhyāyo'dhyetavyaḥ*" - one's *Veda* must be studied. The study of the *Vedas* enables one to pass on that knowledge to the next generation. Therefore, the scriptures also enjoin teaching as one's duty. *Brahma-yajña*, thus, refers to the study and teaching of one's branch of the *Veda*.

Pitṛ Yajña

Pitṛ yajña refers to offering oblation to one's ancestors. One owes them a debt for one's birth and family heritage. This debt is repaid by daily prayers and a ritual called *tarpaṇa*. In *tarpaṇa*, one invokes one's ancestors mentally and makes a physical offering of *tila*, black sesame seeds mixed with rice and *udaka*, water.

Deva Yajña

Deva-yajña is offering daily worship to the gods in recognition of their presence in the laws and functions that govern the universe. Worship of these presiding deities is in the form of a fire ritual called *homa*. In a *homa*, one invokes the deity of fire in a fire altar that is lit according to specific scriptural rules. Unto the fire one makes offerings to various deities, while chanting prayers and *mantras*. One requests the deity of fire to carry the offerings to the deities who are invoked.

Bhūta Yajña

Bhūta-yajña, feeding other living beings, is an act of worship that involves sensitivity to other forms of life. Feeding the hungry is considered a noble and charitable act in most cultures. In the Vedic culture, it is also an act of worship. As part of one's daily duties, one gives food to other living beings, including animals and birds.

In the morning, it is customary for the woman of the house to make decorative designs, called kolam or rangoli, at the entrance to the house. Usually made with powdered rice, these designs welcome the Lord into the house. They also provide food to ants and other small creatures.

Atithi Yajña

Reverence towards guests is highly valued in the Vedic tradition. A guest, whether invited or unexpected, is the recipient of hospitality. If one invites a guest, one can make preparations to be a good host. However, sometimes a guest comes unexpectedly. Before the advent of telecommunications, a guest was more likely to show up unannounced. A guest who comes unannounced is called *atithi* in Sanskrit. The word '*atithi*' means "*tithiḥ na vidyate yasya*" - the one for whom there is no appointed time, or "*aṭati gacchati na tiṣṭhati*" - the one who comes, does not stay behind but leaves. The word '*atithi*' thus refers to a traveller.

The *Manu Smṛti* (3.102) gives a detailed meaning of the term *atithi*:

एकरात्रं तु निवसन्नतिथिर्ब्राह्मणः स्मृतः ।
अनित्यं हि स्थितो यस्मात्तस्मादतिथिरुच्यते ॥

ekarātraṃ tu nivasannatithirbrāhmaṇaḥ smṛtaḥ
anityaṃ hi stitho yasmāttasmād atithirucyate

ekarātram - one night; *tu* - only; *nivasan* - staying; *atithiḥ* - a guest; *brāhmaṇaḥ* - brahmin; *smṛtaḥ*- is known; *anityaṃ* - temporary; *hi* - indeed; *stithaḥ* - stays; *yasmāt* - because; *tasmāt* - therefore; *atithiḥ* - a guest; *ucyate* - is said to be

"A brahmin is called an *atithi* when he stays only for one night. Because he stays temporarily, indeed, he is said to be an *atithi*."

Manu further prescribes the etiquette for relating to a guest, including how to receive and serve a guest, especially a learned person. It requires resilience to handle an unexpected guest. One may have to change one's plans or give up some comforts to accommodate the guest. When one can plan in advance, the mind has an opportunity to adjust to the situation. Adapting to unexpected situations requires much effort and gracefulness.

It is customary to extend hospitality to one's guests by offering them food. Everyone finds it easier to share food with known rather than unknown people. The following verse describes *atithi-yajña* in terms of sharing food:

अज्ञातकुलगोत्रो वा मध्याह्नादिसमागतः ।
अन्नाद्यर्थी मानवो यः सोऽतिथिः परिकीर्तितः ।।

ajñātakulagotro vā madhyānhādi-samāgataḥ
annādyarthī mānavo yaḥ so'tithiḥ parikīrtitaḥ

ajñātakulagotraḥ - the one whose lineage is unknown; *vā* - or; *madhyāhnādi-samāgataḥ* - the one who arrives mid-day, etc.; *annādyarthī* - desiring food; *mānavaḥ* - a person; *yaḥ* - the one who; *saḥ* - that one; *atithiḥ* - a guest; *parikīrtitaḥ* - is said to be

"The person whose lineage is unknown or the one who arrives at mid-day, etc., asking for food, is known as an *atithi*, guest."

Even today in India, there are people who will eat their meal only after serving an *atithi*. This attitude of hospitality and sharing with an unexpected guest, or an unknown person, helps one develop resilience and accommodation.

EXERCISE

I. Unscramble the word to complete the sentence.

1. One invokes one's ancestors mentally and offers oblations in a ritual called *MṆPATRAA* __________________.

2. The decorative designs at the entrance of one's home known as *IORNALG* __________________ is an act of *bhūta-yajña.*

3. Hospitality towards an unexpected guest is known as an *HTITAI* __________________ *yajña.*

4. The Lord looked upon as a presiding deity of a cosmic law is known as a *ĀEAVDT* __________________.

5. *HARMBA* __________________ *yajña* refers to the study and teaching of one's branch of the *Vedas.*

II. True or False. *Check one.*

1. The five daily sacrifices reveal one's sensitivity to the environment. [T] [F]

2. Debts to one's ancestors are repaid through *pitṛ-yajña*. [T] [F]

3. Disrespect towards guests is highly valued in Vedic tradition. [T] [F]

4. An *atithi* is one who visits your home and moves in. [T] [F]

5. In the Vedic culture feeding the hungry is not only a charitable act, but an act of worship to the Lord. [T] [F]

III. Points to Ponder:

1. Have you ever done *bhūta-yajña* (offering food to birds and animals)? What did feeding other creatures mean to you?

____

____

____

____

2. Recall a few times in your life when you felt grateful to the Lord for something you were given.

____

____

____

____

SALUTATION TO THE SUN DEITY

The sun, being the life sustaining force of this planet, is worshipped by the Vedic culture as well as by other ancient cultures around the world. The sun is worshipped for the warmth, energy and light it continuously provides for all the living beings. In the Vedic vision, worship of the sun is worship of *Īśvara*, the Lord, in the form of the sun and its functions. As an object of this worship the sun becomes the sun deity, called *Sūrya-devatā*.

That the sun rises day after day is part of the order we call *Īśvara*. As the sun rises in the sky the whole world becomes active. The chirping birds seem to welcome the sun, the dewdrops shine with the glow of sunlight, the flowers open and share their beauty and fragrance while the plants draw their energy from sunlight. This gift of life and its beauties is received with humility and devotion by those who wake up before dawn and welcome the sun deity with a prayer.

One of the prayers offered to the sun deity is:

जपाकुसुमसंकाशं काश्यपेयं महाद्युतिम् ।
तमोऽरिं सर्वपापघ्नं प्रणतोऽस्मि दिवाकरम् ॥

japākusuma saṃkāśaṃ kāśyapeyaṃ mahādyutim
tamo'riṃ sarvapāpghnaṃ praṇato'smi divākaram

japākusuma saṃkāśam - like the resplendent *japā* flower (hibiscus); *kāśyapeyam*- son of Sage *Kaśyapa*; *mahādyutim* - brilliant; *tamo'rim* - the enemy (destroyer) of darkness; *sarva-pāpghnaṃ* - destroyer of the results of wrong actions; *praṇataḥ asmi* - I salute; *divākaram* - the sun deity

"I salute the sun deity, who is resplendent like the *japā* flower, who is the son of Sage *Kaśyapa*, who is brilliant, who is the enemy of darkness, and who is the destroyer of the results of wrong actions."

The *Gāyatrī-mantra* is an important prayer dedicated to the sun deity. In this *mantra* one prays for brilliance and knowledge.*

In the *yoga* literature various *āsanas*, physical postures, are described. These *āsanas* are performed as an exercise for the well-being of one's body and mind. One such *āsana* is called *sūrya-namaskāra*, prostration to the sun. The physical posture is accompanied by a prayer to the sun deity, which consists of twelve *mantras*. Sequentially, one *mantra* is chanted for every salutation and a total of twelve salutations are performed.

The twelve *mantras* are :

1) ॐ मित्राय नमः। *oṃ mitrāya namaḥ*

Prostrations to him who is friendly to all.

2) ॐ रवये नमः। *oṃ ravaye namaḥ*

Prostrations to him who is the cause for change.

3) ॐ सूर्याय नमः। *oṃ sūryāya namaḥ*

Prostrations to him who propels everyone into activity.

4) ॐ भानवे नमः। *oṃ bhānave namaḥ*

Prostrations to him who is in the form of light.

5) ॐ खगाय नमः। *oṃ khagāya namaḥ*

Prostrations to him who moves in the sky.

6) ॐ पूष्णे नमः। *oṃ pūṣṇe namaḥ*

Prostrations to him who nourishes all.

7) ॐ हिरण्यगर्भाय नमः। *oṃ hiraṇyagarbhāya namaḥ*

Prostrations to him who contains everything.

8) ॐ मरीचये नमः। *oṃ marīcaye namaḥ*

Prostrations to him who possesses rays.

9) ॐ आदित्याय नमः। *oṃ ādityāya namaḥ*

Prostrations to him who is the son of *Aditi*.

10) ॐ सवित्रे नमः। *oṃ savitre namaḥ*

Prostrations to him who produces everything.

11) ॐ अर्काय नमः। *oṃ arkāya namaḥ*

Prostrations to him who is fit to be worshipped.

12) ॐ भास्कराय नमः। *oṃ bhāskarāya namaḥ*

Prostrations to him who is the cause of lustre.

The worship of the *Sūrya-devatā* is a common and important expression of devotion to the Lord.

* Refer to "*Sandhyāvandanam*", Part 7.

EXERCISE

I. Fill in the blanks with the words below to complete each sentence.

yoga	*Gāyatrī*	before
after	*Kaśyapa*	Sun God

1. ________________ *mantra* is an important prayer dedicated to the Sun God.
2. *Sūrya-namaskāra* is taught as an *āsana* in the ________________ literature.
3. In the *purāṇas* the Sun God is looked upon as the son of Sage ________________.
4. In the *Mahābhārata*, *Karṇa* was the son of the ________________.
5. In the religious culture of India, one wakes up ________________ dawn as a mark of respect to the Sun God.

II. Points to Ponder:

1. List three reasons why one should be grateful to the Sun God.

____

____

2. Can you think of any other culture in the world that looks upon the Sun as a deity? Share it with the class.

____

____

III. Practise at home.

Learn how to do the Salutation to the Sun. Chant one of these twelve names of the Sun in the given order before each salutation. Do this Salutation twelve times.

1. *oṃ mitrāya namaḥ*
   Prostration to Him who is friendly to all.

2. *oṃ ravaye namaḥ*
   Prostration to Him who is the cause for change.

3. *oṃ sūryāya namaḥ*
   Prostration to Him who propels everyone into activity.

4. *oṃ bhānave namaḥ*
   Prostration to Him who is in the form of light.

5. *oṃ khagāya namaḥ*
   Prostration to Him who moves in the sky.

6. *oṃ pūṣṇe namaḥ*
   Prostration to Him who nourishes all.

7. *oṃ hiraṇyagarbhāya namaḥ*
   Prostration to Him who contains everything.

8. *oṃ marīcaye namaḥ*
   Prostration to Him who possesses rays.

9. *oṃ ādityāya namaḥ*
   Prostration to Him who is the son of *Aditi*.

10. *oṃ savitre namaḥ*
    Prostration to Him who produces everything.

11. *oṃ arkāya namaḥ*
    Prostration to Him who is fit to be worshipped.

12. *oṃ bhāskarāya namaḥ*
    Prostration to Him who is the cause of lustre.

Salutation to the Sun

SANDHYĀVANDANAM

In the Vedic way of life, worship of *Īśvara* in the form of the sun deity occupies an important place. The sun is the source of life giving energy and sustenance. One expresses one's gratitude to the sun deity by offering prayers unto him.

One *nitya-karma*, daily duty, mandated by the *Vedas* is *Sandhyāvandana*. The *Veda* states, "*aharahar sandhyāmupāsīta*" - one should worship the Lord daily during *sandhyā*. The word '*sandhyā*', derived from the Sanskrit root '*dhyai*- to meditate', means the Lord. The word '*vandana*' means salutation. *Sandhyāvandana* refers to salutation to the Lord. The word '*sandhyā*' also derives from the word '*sandhi*', which means union and refers to the time of joining of the night and day, as well as the forenoon and afternoon. Hence *sandhyā* refers to dawn, noon and dusk. At these three times, the *Vedas* enjoin one to perform *sandhyāvandana*.

Sandhyāvandana is a ritual with many steps, including external and internal purification; meditation on Lord *Gaṇeśa*; offering water to *Sūrya-devatā*; offering *arghya*, oblations, to the planets and other deities; and doing *Gāyatrī-japa*. The *Gāyatrī-mantra* is chanted a minimum of 108 times at dawn, thirty-two times at noon and sixty-four times at dusk. The *sandhyāvandana* ends with prayers to *devatās*, including *Yamarājā* and *Sūrya-nārāyaṇa* (*Viṣṇu*).

Gāyatrī (*Sāvitrī*) *Mantra*

The *Gāyatrī-mantra* is a Vedic *mantra* (*Ṛg Veda*, 3.62.10) which is considered to be a highly efficacious prayer. As it is a prayer to *Savitā*, the sun deity, it is also called the *Sāvitrī-mantra*. The *Gāyatrī-mantra* is in the meter called *gāyatrī*, which is made up of twenty-four syllables in three parts of eight syllables each.* This *mantra* is popularly known after the meter in which it is recited. Similar prayers to the sun deity occur in other meters, including *anuṣṭubh*, *triṣṭubh* and *jagatī*, but in the *Bṛhadāraṇyaka Upaniṣad* (5.14.5) there is mandate that says the *Gāyatrī-mantra* is to be recited in the *gāyatrī* meter alone.

The Meaning of *Gāyatrī*

The *Gāyatrī-mantra* is as follows:

ॐ भूर्भुवस्सुवः। तत सवितुर्वरेण्यम् ।
भर्गो देवस्य धीमहि । धियो यो नः प्रचोदयात् ॥

oṃ bhūrbhuvassuvaḥ / tat saviturvareṇyam
bhargo devasya dhīmahi / dhiyo yo naḥ pracodayāt

oṃ bhūrbhuvassuvaḥ - *Om* is the basis of everything; *tat* - that Lord; *savituḥ* - of the sun; *vareṇyam* - the most worshipped; *bhargaḥ* - who is all-knowing; *devasya* - of the Lord; *dhīmahi* - we meditate; *dhiyaḥ* - intellects; *yaḥ* - the one; *naḥ* - our; *pracodayāt* - may he set in the right direction or may he brighten

"*Om*, is the basis of everything. That Lord is the one who is the most worshipful. We meditate on that all-knowing Lord. May he set our intellects in the right direction."

The first line, *oṃ bhūrbhuvassuvaḥ*, is technically not part of the twenty-four syllables of the *mantra*. In this line, the word '*Om*' is the name for *Īśvara*, the Lord. *Bhūḥ* refers to the universe. *Bhuvaḥ* refers to all possible worlds above that are not seen, and *suvaḥ* refers to the heavens. Thus, the three words *bhūrbhuvassuvaḥ* refer to everything seen and unseen. The meaning of the sentence is that all the worlds, seen and unseen, are nothing but *Īśvara*.

The meaning of the rest of the *mantra* is as follows:

tad vareṇyam - "That (Lord) is worshipful".

(*tasya*) *devasya savituḥ dhīmahi* - "We meditate (on) that (all-knowing) effulgence of the deity of sun (Lord)".

yaḥ bhargaḥ naḥ dhiyaḥ pracodayāt - "May that effulgent (one) illumine our intellects."

Gāyatrī: *Mahāvākya* and Prayer

A *mahāvākya* is a sentence that reveals the identity between the individual and the Lord. A *mahāvākya* thus predicates an equation between two variables. In the *Gāyatrī-mantra*, that which is the cause of everything is indicated by the syllable *Om*, which means the Lord. The essential nature of the Lord is equated to the self in the form of limitless awareness. By understanding the meaning of the *Gāyatrī-mantra*, one can appreciate the identity of the individual with the Lord.

As a prayer, this *mantra* is addressed to the deity presiding over the sun, which is looked upon as being worshipful. One prays to the Lord in the form of the sun for clarity of intellect so that the intellect may be an effective instrument for learning. Thus the *Gāyatrī-mantra* can be a prayer and also, when understood, a *mahāvākya*.

Praise of *Gāyatrī*

The *Upaniṣad* and the *Purāṇas* glorify *Gāyatrī* by describing it as the greatest of *mantras*. The *Chāndogya Upaniṣad* (3.12.1) gives the meaning of the *Gāyatrī-mantra* and praises it as follows: "*gāyati ca trāyate ca*" - it sings and protects. *Gāyatrī* sings because it is in meter form. It protects in two ways. Being a prayer, it protects a person by creating an attitude of devotion and acceptance. As a *mahāvākya*, it protects one from sorrow and limitation by giving one self-knowledge. The *Mahānārāyaṇa Upaniṣad* (15.1) states: "*gāyatrīṃ chandasāṃ mātā*", meaning "the *gāyatrī* meter which is the mother among the meters", or "the *Gāyatrī-mantra* which is the mother among the *Vedas*". In the *Bhagavad Gītā* (10.35) Lord *Kṛṣṇa* praises *gāyatrī* when he says, "*gāyatrī chandasām aham*" - among the meters, I am the *gāyatrī*. Because of its efficacy as a prayer and as a *mahāvākya*, *Gāyatrī* is considered to be the essence of the *Vedas*.

Initiation into *Gāyatrī*

In the Vedic culture, one's study of the scriptures begins with the *saṃskāra* of *upanayana*.** In this ritual, the student is initiated into the *Gāyatrī-mantra* either by his father or by his teacher. *Gāyatrī* thus sanctifies the beginning of life as a *Brahmacārī*, student.

* Refer to "Prosody", Part 11.

** Refer to "The Sixteen *Saṃskāras*", Part 9.

EXERCISE

I. Answer these questions:

1. Why is *sandhyāvandana* mandated by the *Vedas* as a *nitya-karma*?

____

____

____

2. What does the word *sandhyāvandana* mean?

____

____

____

3. Which *mantra* is chanted to gain intelligence and maturity?

____

____

____

4. Name the ritual in which a child is initiated into *Gāyatrī*.

____

____

____

5. In simple words, give the meaning of the *Gāyatrī-mantra*.

____

____

____

II. A Quiz on *Gāyatrī* *Fill in the blanks with the words below to complete each sentence.*

protects	mother	24-syllable	teacher
meters	20-syllable	*Gāyatrī*	Sun God

1. In the *Bhagavad Gītā* the Lord says among the ________________ I am *Gāyatrī*.
2. The *Mahānārāyaṇa Upaniṣad* praises *Gāyatrī* as the ________________ of the *Vedas*.
3. *Gāyatrī* is a prayer that ________________ the one who sings it.
4. *Gāyatrī* is a prayer dedicated to the ________________.
5. *Gāyatrī-mantra* is always chanted in ________________ meter.
6. *Gāyatrī* is a ________________ *mantra*.

III. Points to Ponder:

1. Have you ever participated in an *upanayana* ritual? Describe how the person was initiated into the *Gāyatrī-mantra*?

____

____

____

2. Spend some time in your *pūjā* room and contemplate upon the meaning of the *Gāyatrī-mantra*. Use this prayer in your own words to seek the blessings of the Lord.

____

____

____

KARMA AS A RELIGIOUS DISCIPLINE

In the Vedic culture certain actions are performed for oneself as mandated by scriptures while other actions are performed for the benefit of society. These actions are classified as *iṣṭa-karmas* and *pūrta-karmas* respectively. In the *dharma-śāstra* (*Manu Smṛti* 4.226-227), one is advised to perform these actions faithfully, with a cheerful disposition and according to one's capacity. When these actions are performed with the right attitude they are conducive to spiritual growth.

Iṣṭa Karmas

Iṣṭa-karmas are actions that are stated in the *Vedas* and are performed mainly for one's benefit. The following verse describes *iṣṭa-karmas*:

अग्निहोत्रं तपः सत्यं वेदानां चानुपालनम् ।
आतिथ्यं वैश्वदेवं च इष्टमित्याभिधीयते ॥

agnihotraṃ tapaḥ satyaṃ vedānāṃ cānupālanam
ātithyaṃ vaiśvadevaṃ ca iṣṭaṃ ityabhidhīyate

agnihotram - *agnihotra* (fire) ritual; *tapaḥ* - austerities; *satyam* - truthfulness; *vedānām*- of the *Vedas*; *ca* - and; *anupālanam* - daily recitation; *ātithyam* - service to the guest; *vaiśvadevam* - *vaiśvadeva* ritual; *ca* - and; *iṣṭam* - *iṣṭa-karma*; *iti* - thus; *abhidhīyate* - is called

"*Agnihotra* ritual, austerities, truthfulness, the daily recitation of the *Vedas*, *vaiśvadeva* ritual and service to the guest are called *iṣṭa-karmas*."

The rituals mentioned here are enjoined by the *Vedas* and *dharma-śāstra*. They are *nitya-karmas*, duties to be done daily, and are to be performed by one who is leading the life of a householder. Performing *nitya-karmas* results in *puṇya*, the unseen results of good actions. These unseen results fructify in situations which are conducive to emotional and spiritual growth.

Pūrta Karmas

Pūrta-karmas are actions that are done for the benefit of society and give one a sense of fulfillment. One may undertake a *pūrta-karma* in keeping with a resolve, *pratijñā*, or as an expiatory act, *Prāyaścitta-karma*. The following verse describes *pūrta-karmas*:

वापीकूपतडागादि देवतायतनानि च ।
अन्नप्रदानमारामः पूर्तमित्यभिधीयते ॥

vāpīkūpataḍāgādi devatāyatanāni ca
annapradānamārāmaḥ pūrtam ityabhidhīyate

vāpīkūpataḍāgādi - tank or reservoir, well, watering holes, etc.; *devatāyatanāni* - temples; *ca* - and; *annapradānam* - feeding the needy; *ārāmaḥ* - rest homes; *pūrtam* - *pūrta-karmas*; *iti* - thus; *abhidhīyate* - are so called

"Constructing tanks or reservoirs, temples, rest homes; digging wells and watering holes; and feeding the needy, etc., are called *pūrta-karmas*."

Digging wells and constructing reservoirs of water in the form of tanks, lakes, or ponds are of great service to humanity. They ensure a constant supply of water to people in areas when the water supply is scarce or seasonal. Similarly, constructing watering holes where animals can also find water is a charitable act indicating sensitivity to one's fellow creatures.

In India, the building of temples and places of worship was mainly undertaken by kings and wealthy people. Temples not only serve as places of prayer and pilgrimage, but create a context wherein people in a given society can spiritually bond. To provide such a place of refuge is considered to be a meritorious act.

Feeding those in need of food is another charitable act that is practised in all cultures. It is an expression of sensitivity to another's need and a genuine willingness to share what one has been given.

In the Vedic society many people undertake pilgrimages to temples and other sacred places. Rest houses are built along the way to make the journeys of the pilgrims more comfortable. Generally these facilities are provided free of cost to the pilgrims. Such rest homes are seen all over India and are widely used.

EXERCISE

I. Define the following words.

1. *iṣṭa-karma*

2. *pūrta-karma*

3. *puṇya*

4. expiatory actions

5. *nitya-karma*

II. Classify the listed actions as *iṣṭa-karma* or *pūrta-karma*.

1. *Agnihotra* ritual ____________________
2. study of *Vedas* ____________________
3. feeding the poor ____________________
4. building reservoirs ____________________
5. truthfulness ____________________
6. building resthouses ____________________
7. building temples ____________________
8. austerities ____________________
9. purity ____________________
10. building wells ____________________

III. Point to Ponder:

Can you think of four more *iṣṭa-karmas* and *pūrta-karmas* that you consider relevant to modern society?

____

____

____

____

____

____

DISCIPLINE IN SPEECH

Vāk-tapas is the discipline of proper use of one's speech. The word '*tapas*' means a religious discipline that is self-imposed for one's own benefit. In the process of developing mastery over speech, one inevitably develops a capacity to master the mind, as speech and the mind are intimately connected. Speech being an instrument of expression, like any instrument, it must be properly handled with alertness.

Speech is not an involuntary function. It is subject to will and therefore can be controlled. Due to habit or lack of alertness, however, it can appear to be mechanical. When speech is mechanical, there is minimum use of will to control or modify it. Whatever thought comes to mind is expressed without regard to propriety or concern for consequences. Careless speech can result in poor communication, hurt feelings and misinterpretations.

The first step in *vāk-tapas* is being alert to one's speech. As words once spoken are irretrievable, it is important to be certain of what one wants to say before speaking. If one's thoughts are vague or confused, they need to be sorted out before one tries to communicate. Then one will not find oneself saying, "I did not mean what I said". Although it is important that one's speech be in keeping with what one thinks, it is not necessary to verbalise everything that one thinks. Speech should be the finished product of one's thinking, not the raw material.

Since thoughts and speech are so intimately connected, alertness to one's speech also brings about an alertness to one's own feelings and process of thinking. To effect change within oneself, one needs to be aware of one's thoughts and emotional patterns. One also needs to be alert to the consequences of what one says, as one's speech can have a lasting impression on others. Discipline in speech implies truthfulness backed by sensitivity towards others.*

In *vāk-tapas*, one avoids talking simply for the sake of talking. Talking serves various functions. It can be a means for getting to know people and interacting with them. However, in the practice of *vāk-tapas*, one deliberately avoids un-productive conversation such as gossip about the affairs of others which are irrelevant to oneself. People indulge in gossip to kill time and satisfy idle curiosity. It can also be destructive, as the information passed on is often coloured by distortions and misconceptions. Having passed through many idle minds, gossip is as far from the truth as it is from its source.

One can also indulge in talking as a way of dealing with loneliness and escaping from one's own uncomfortable thoughts and feelings. When talking becomes a form of escape and avoidance, it may be of use momentarily, but in the long run does not lead to inner growth.

Types of Discussion

Speech in the form of discussion is an important instrument for learning. By discussion, one can develop thoughts more fully and clarify doubts. Unproductive discussion, however, should be avoided. The Vedic tradition describes three types of discussion:

1) *Jalpa* - In this form of discussion, the proponents on each side firmly stick to their position and try to convince their opponents, refusing to see the other viewpoint even if it appears more reasonable. The purpose of the discussion is not to seek what is true, but to impose an opinion on others. It is like a discussion between believers of different religious groups or political parties.

2) *Vitaṇḍā* - In this form of discussion also, each side sticks firmly to their view, but they argue by contesting and debating everything that the other side says. The intent is to disagree, and not to reach

an understanding regarding the matter discussed. This type of discussion reflects a clash of personalities and egotistical behaviour.

3) *Vāda* - In this form of discussion, those on each side may take a position, but their main purpose is to understand the truth. Each side is willing to listen to the other and change their viewpoint to what seems reasonable. This type of discussion is appropriate for those who follow the discipline of *vāk-tapas* and who are open minded and ready to learn.

By practising *vāk-tapas*, one develops an alertness to one's speech and thoughts. One also becomes aware of one's process of thinking, which helps in developing clarity of thought. This clarity is a powerful aid to emotional growth.

* Refer to "Truthfulness", Part 6.

EXERCISE

I. Unscramble the word to complete each sentence.

1. The first step in *vāk-tapas* is being ETARL ________________ to one's speech.

2. Being attentive to one's speech brings about an alertness in one's HNIGNKIT ________________ process.

3. When one is alert to one's thinking process, one can bring about a healthy GACHNE ________________ in oneself.

4. In the practice of *vāk-tapas* one deliberately avoids PSOGSI ________________.

5. Of the three forms of discussion, *DVĀA* ________________ alone is fruitful.

6. *Vāk-tapas* is the practice of speech that is ULRUFTHT ________________ kind and meaningful.

II. Points to Ponder:

1. What happens to words once they are uttered? Is there any way to take them back?

2. Is it better to say whatever comes to your mind or to think about what comes to your mind before saying it? Why?

3. Is anything gained by gossiping?

III. Journal Writing

1. Write about one episode when you indulged in

   a) *jalpa*

   b) *vitaṇḍā*

   c) *vāda*

2. Write about the times you indulged in gossip during the week.

   a. Think about what was said and how you would feel if those things were being said about you.

   b. Think about whether the person that was being talked about would be hurt by what was said.

ACTS OF CHARITY

In Vedic culture, charity, *dāna*, is looked upon as a religious discipline. Many *Upaniṣads*, such as the *Bṛhadāraṇyaka Upaniṣad* (4.4.22), the *Chāndogya Upaniṣad* (2.23.1) and the *Mahānārāyaṇa Upaniṣad* (21.2) extol the virtues of *dāna* as a religious duty.

The *Bhagavad Gītā* (18.5) describes *dāna* as one of the three means of purifying one's mind, the other two being *yajña*, Vedic rituals; and *tapas*, austerities. *Dāna* is also considered to be a daily obligatory duty of a Hindu. In order to cultivate this value in people, there are many occasions and situations that are considered to be auspicious for giving charity and many forms by which it is given.

Occasions for Charity

Birth - Birth is a time for rejoicing. It marks the beginning of an individual's life and is a time of happiness for the parents and family. This joy is shared with others in the form of giving charity.

Sixtieth Birthday - The sixtieth birthday is considered to be an important milestone in one's life. Astrologically, it takes sixty years for the constellations to arrive at the same position they did at the time of one's birth. This event represents the completion of one cycle in one's life. Furthermore, the person offers prayers to the Lord and gives different forms of charity.

Death - This is a significant and final event in an individual's life. Charity is given in the name of the departed so that *puṇya* may accrue to the individual to proceed onward without impediments in his or her journey.

Eclipse - Both the solar and lunar eclipses are significant events from an astrological stand-point. They are unusual occurrences in nature and evoke awe in people. They are also seen to affect other forms of life. In order to prevent any harmful effects that might occur during this time, charity is given.

Seasons - There are certain months during the year that are considered auspicious for giving charity. One significant time is *Śrāvaṇa* (July-August), the lunar month which brings rains. Rains are the very life of an agricultural society like India, and so this month represents the coming of prosperity. Another significant period for giving charity is the month of *Mārgaśira*, (November-December). This is the time when nature in her many forms becomes particularly vibrant. In describing the glories of his creation in the *Bhagavad Gītā* (10.35), Lord *Kṛṣṇa* describes himself as *Mārgaśira* among all the months of the year.

Places - Any place of pilgrimage or place of worship is considered an auspicious place for giving charity. One place where people commonly give charity is *Kurukṣetra*, where the *Mahābhārata* war took place. At *Kurukṣetra*, *adharma* was defeated and *dharma* re-established. Thus, giving charity here is believed to alleviate one from past *pāpa-karmas*.

Forms of Charity

Even though one has the freedom to give charity in any form, there are certain forms of charity which are culturally significant to a Hindu. Some of these include:

Anna-dāna - Giving *anna*, food, as charity is considered to be a noble act. Food is an object that gives a sense of fullness, *alaṃbuddhi*, to the received. One of the five daily sacrifices* that a person is supposed to perform daily is called *nṛ-yajña*, also known as *atithi-yajña*, receiving the guest. In this ritual one eats only after feeding another person. This practice is meant to instil the value of sharing.

Anna-dāna is a step in most rituals. One of the rituals in which it is a significant act is the *vājapeya-yajña*. In India, there are many temples and *Gurudvāras* where hundreds of people are fed every day.

Kanyā-dāna - This is a beautiful and poignant concept in the Vedic culture. Of the many things that a parent may have, the child is the most treasured. While raising a child, a parent develops intense attachment to him or her. When a daughter gets married she usually leaves her home to join the husband's family. This event is an occasion for mixed feelings in her parents; joy at the new beginning of their daughter's life and the sorrow of separation from her. When the parents give their daughter's hand in marriage, it is a moment of deep loss as they are giving away one who is most treasured. A Vedic marriage ceremony includes a step known as *kanyā-dāna*, giving away of one's daughter in marriage. People feel blessed if they can perform *kanyā-dāna* during their lifetime.

Go-dāna - *Go-dāna* is giving cows as charity. In an agricultural society such as India, cows are looked upon as wealth. One or more cows are given as charity during certain occasions such as *ṣaṣṭyabdhapūrti*, the sixtieth birthday; and *antyeṣṭi-karma*, a ritual done for the departed immediately after death.

Vidyā-dāna - In the Vedic culture, knowledge was always given in the form of charity. Neither knowledge nor food was ever sold, they were freely shared with others. A student lived with and served his teacher who, in turn, gave him knowledge. Both were supported by the society. Even though this practice is not prevalent today, it still exists in imparting spiritual knowledge and knowledge of fine and performing arts.

Bhū-dāna and *Gṛha-dāna* - *Bhū-dāna* is giving land. This is usually done by the wealthy. Those who own land or other immovable properties, like buildings and houses, give the same to the needy. Sometimes land is endowed to a temple to help sustain its needs. *Gṛha-dāna* is giving a house or shelter as charity to one in need.

Vastra-dāna and *Svarṇa-dāna* - *Vastra-dāna* is giving clothes as charity. It is done on joyful occasions, such as the birth of a child; certain festivals, like *Navarātri*; and at the time of the solar or lunar eclipse. *Svarṇa-dāna* is giving gold as charity. It is done in keeping with one's means on occasions such as a wedding or the birth of a child.

Dhānya-dāna and *Jala-dāna* - Other necessities, such as grains, *dhānya*; and water, *jala*, can be given as charity. Food may be given to the needy in the form of grains. Farmers sometimes make a resolve to give a certain portion of their produce as charity. *Jala-dāna* is in the form of providing a source of water for people and animals, and is one of the *pūrta-karmas*. Providing fresh cold water to weary pilgrims and travellers is considered to be a blessing to both the receiver and the giver.**

Abhaya-dāna - *Abhaya-dāna* is giving fearlessness in the form of charity. At the time of taking *sannyāsa*, a Hindu monk gives *abhaya-dāna* to all living beings by taking a vow of *ahiṃsā*, noninjury and by living a lifestyle of non-competitiveness.

In giving charity one is not restricted to time or place. Even though the above occasions are considered to be auspicious, one can give charity at any time and any place.

* Refer to "The Five Daily Sacrifices", Part 7.

** Refer to "*Karma* as a Religious Discipline", Part 7.

EXERCISE

I. Complete these sentences in your own words.

1. One gives to charity because...

2. When I give to charity, I feel...

3. I like to give to a cause I believe in because...

4. Charity is sharing...

5. The occasions for charity are...

II. True or False. *Check one.*

1.	The *Bhagavad Gītā* describes charity along withVedic rituals and austerities as means of purifying one's mind.	T	F
2.	Charity is not looked upon as a religious discipline.	T	F
3.	The duration of an eclipse is seen as an auspicious time for giving.	T	F
4.	One place especially noted for giving charity is *Kurukṣetra.*	T	F
5.	One has the freedom to give charity in any form.	T	F
6.	In the Vedic culture, knowledge is never sold.	T	F
7.	A person's sixty-fifth birthday is considered to be an important milestone in Vedic culture.	T	F
8.	In India, many temples feed people every day.	T	F
9.	Giving charity is considered to be a monthly obligatory duty	T	F.
10.	*Śrāvaṇa* and *Mārgaśira* are considered to be auspicious months of the year for giving charity.	T	F

III. Identify these forms of *dāna*.

anna-dāna	*kanyā-dāna*	*go-dāna*	*gṛha-dāna*
vidyā-dāna	*bhū-dāna*	*jala-dāna*	*abhaya-dāna*

1. Donating books to a library is ____________________.

2. Feeding the poor is ____________________.

3. Donating land to a temple is ____________________.

4. Giving one's daughter away in marriage is ____________________.

5. Donating cows to the temple in memory of a dear one is ____________________.

6. Giving shelter to one in need is ____________________.

7. Giving land to build an ashram is ____________________.

8. Taking a vow of *ahiṃsā* is ____________________.

9. Building a reservoir to provide water for a village is ____________________.

10. Giving knowledge is ____________________.

IV. Points to Ponder:

1. What charities do you consider to be the most worthwhile? Why?

2. Giving food is one act of charity that is found in almost all cultures. What is the reason for this?

3. Why do you think that one never paid for knowledge in Vedic society?

4. Why does charity begin at home?

RELIGIOUS PURITY

The *dharma-śāstra* prescribes certain codes of conduct which help one develop important attitudes in one's life. These codes of conduct are known as *ācāras*. One observes *ācāras* by performing certain actions which are considered to make one religiously pure. These purifying actions are defined as "*vaidika-karma-yogyatā-sampādaka-vyāpāraḥ*" - an action that brings about eligibility for performing *karmas* enjoined in the *Vedas*.

The following are some purificatory actions:

Ācamana

Ācamana is the first step in performing any Vedic ritual. Through *ācamana*, one sanctifies oneself in order to be eligible to perform worship. *Ācamana* is defined in Sanskrit as "*vāra-traya-jala-pānam; tad-anantaraṃ yathākramam aṣṭāṅga-sparśa-rūpa-śuddhi-janaka-kriyā*"- sipping water three times and thereafter touching eight points of the body in given order, thus sanctifying (oneself).

Performing *ācamana* One pours a small amount of water in the palm of the right hand and sips it. This is done three times; the first time chanting "*om acyutāya namaḥ*" - salutations to the unchangeable one; then "*om anantāya namaḥ*" - salutations to the limitless one; and lastly "*oṃ govindāya namaḥ*" - salutations to the one who is revealed by the *Vedas*. One then touches the following parts of one's upper body with fingers of the right hand while repeating these *mantras*:

Right and left cheeks with the thumb, chanting '*Keśava, Nārāyaṇa*'.

Right and left eyes with the ring finger, chanting '*Mādhava, Govinda*'.

Right and left nostrils with the index finger chanting '*Viṣṇu, Madhusūdana*'.

Right and left ears with the little finger chanting '*Trivikrama, Vāmana*'.

Right and left shoulder with the middle finger chanting '*Śrīdhara, Hṛṣīkeśa*'.

The chest with all fingers chanting '*Padmanābha*', and touching the top of the head chanting '*Dāmodara*'.

By these actions one invokes the presence of various deities in oneself and begins any worship.

Darbha

Darbha is an instrument of purification. It is a kind of grass that is used while performing Vedic rituals. It is used to sanctify items that are connected with worship. When it is worn on the ring finger of the right hand with prescribed *mantras* it is called *pavitra* and serves to sanctify the person.

Madi

Washing and wearing one's clothes in a particular manner one maintains madi, religious purity, until one completes one's daily *pūjā*. In observing madi, it is necessary that one is not touched by anyone who has not gone through the same procedure of madi.

Snāna One of the ways by which one maintains religious purity is by *snāna*, a purificatory bath. There are five types of *snāna* which are connected to the use of the five elements: *ākāśa*, space; *vāyu*, air; *agni*, fire; *āpaḥ*, water; and *pṛthivī*, earth. They are as follows:

1) *Varuṇa-snāna*: a bath associated with water

This *snāna*, which is the most common, is five-limbed and is described in the following verse:

सङ्कल्पस्सूक्तपठनं मार्जनं चाघमर्षणम् ।
देवतातर्पणं चैव स्नानं पञ्चाङ्गमुच्यते ॥

saṅkalpassūktapaṭhanaṃ mārjanaṃ cāghamarṣaṇam
devatātarpaṇaṃ caiva snānaṃ pañcāṅgamucyate

saṅkalpaḥ - the mention of intent; *sūktapaṭhanam* - chanting Vedic prayers; *mārjanam* - sprinkling water on oneself; *ca* - and; *aghamarṣaṇam* - taking a bath, chanting specific *mantras*; *devatā-tarpaṇam* - offering oblations to the deities; *ca* - and; *eva* - indeed; *snānam* - purificatory bath; *pañcāṅgam* - five-limbed; *ucyate* - is called

"The five-limbed purificatory bath consists of mentioning the intent, chanting Vedic prayers, sprinkling water on oneself, taking a bath chanting specific *mantras* and offering oblations to the deities."

2) *Mantra-snāna*: a bath associated with *mantras*

In this *snāna* one sprinkles water on oneself while chanting specific *mantras*. Since *mantras* are in the form of sounds and sound travels through space, this *snāna* is associated with the element space.

3) *Vibhūti-snāna*: a bath associated with sacred ash

In this *snāna*, one purifies oneself by applying *vibhūti*, sacred ash, all over the body. This *snāna* is also called *āgneya-snāna*, a bath associated with fire, since the ash is obtained from fire.

4) *Divya-snāna*: a bath associated with the heavens

Taking a bath by drenching oneself in the rain which occurs while the sun is shining is considered purificatory. It is as if the rain is blessed by the sun. This is an unusual occurrence as generally the sun is covered by clouds when it rains.

5) *Vāyavya-snāna*: a bath associated with air

Here the *snāna* involves placing upon oneself dust that is stirred up by the feet of cows. This dust is called *go-dhūli*. Air and earth are the elements associated with this *snāna*.

Some of the other acts that bring about religious purity are wearing the sacred thread; wearing a *mālā* of *rudrākṣa* or other sacred beads; and applying *vibhūti*, sacred ash, or *candana*, sandalwood paste, on one's forehead.

Religious Impurity

Even though one may maintain religious purity in one's daily life, certain situations still arise that impute religious impurities to an individual. In observing religious codes of conduct, one honours these situations that bring about religious impurity for a length of time. After the prescribed time has lapsed, one takes a symbolic purificatory bath which releases oneself from the impurity.

The *dharma-śāstra* imputes religious impurity in certain situations. It is important to know that impurity is not literal or derogatory, but attitudinal. Certain situations are considered to give rise to religious impurity because of their association with sorrow, pain or discomfort. Pain and sorrow are believed to be the result of wrong actions and therefore are associated with impurity. Some examples of religious impurity are as follows:

1) Upon the death of a person, the immediate family is considered impure for ten days.

2) Following the birth of a child, the parents are considered impure for ten days. This is known as *sūdaka* or *jananāśauca*.

3) In a place where eclipse is cited, one is considered to acquire religious impurity for the duration of the eclipse.

4) A woman is considered impure during the time of her menstrual period.

Religious impurities are seen in varying degrees. The death of a person, for example, brings sorrow to family members, and thus the religious impurity arising from death is considered at a maximum. The birth of a child, on the other hand, being an occasion for joy, has relatively less religious impurity. Even though the time of eclipse makes one impure, it is considered to be specially auspicious time for *japa*, and thus the degree of impurity is minimal. The impurity of the menstrual period is limited to the first three days during which time the woman refrains from performing *pūjās*.

The observance of religious impurity during the menstrual period is commonly practised by women even today. The woman is considered impure for herself and others. If a person happens to touch her customarily that individual takes a bath before performing his religious duties. During this time the woman also refrains from cooking since the food cooked at home is always offered to the Lord as part of one's daily *pūjā*. It is as though the *dharma-śāstra* has given the woman a rest for three days to regain her physical and emotional strength before she continues her daily chores during other times of the month.

Living a life according to the religious codes of conduct leads one to a life of alertness and self-discipline. These religious codes of conduct also help one discover an appreciation of the beauty inherent in living a Vedic way of life.

EXERCISE

I. Circle the odd one out.

1. *Ācamana* is an act of
   a) purification
   b) quenching one's thirst
   c) performing the first step in any ritual

2. *Ācāras* refer to
   a) religious codes of conduct
   b) the subject matter of the *dharma-śāstra*
   c) one's spiritual teachers

3. According to the *dharma-śāstra*, death gives rise to religious impurity for the bereaved because of
   a) the anger it brings
   b) its association with sorrow
   c) the disintegration of the body

4. One may release oneself from a religious impurity by
   a) committing suicide
   b) taking a purificatory bath
   c) performing an act of atonement

5. When a woman has her menstrual period it is a common custom
   a) to refrain from cooking
   b) to refrain from performing *pūjās*
   c) to celebrate those days with family members

II. List the words appropriately.

sacred ash	*mantra-snāna*
darbha grass	*rudrākṣa* beads
ācamana	sacred thread
Prāyaścitta-karma	chanting the Lord's name

1. PURIFICATORY MATERIALS

____

____

____

____

2. PURIFICATORY ACTS

____

____

____

____

III. Points to Ponder:

1. Why is it difficult to follow an *ācāra*, discipline, if you don't understand what it means?

___

___

___

2. What are some of the *ācāras* that you follow?

___

___

___

3. Identify one *ācāra* that your parent or grandparent observes. What does its observance mean to him or her?

___

___

___

IV. Field Work

Find out some of the "kosher" practices of the Jewish tradition. See how they compare with the *ācāras* of the Hindu tradition.

___

___

___

EIGHT-LIMBED YOGA

To live a life of contentment, one must necessarily be in harmony with oneself and the world. This includes a balance in the physical, psychological and social aspects of one's life. *Aṣṭāṅga-yoga* provides a systematic combination of disciplines and attitudes to enable one to live a harmonious life. It is a complete system of eightfold disciplines described by *Patañjali*. Written in the form of aphorisms, *sūtras*, these disciplines help one achieve a state of physical and mental well-being.

The first two disciplines, *yama* and *niyama*, describe the healthy disposition of a human being and form the basis of the practice of the remaining six disciplines. *Āsana* and *prāṇāyāma*, the third and the fourth disciplines, discuss right posture and regulation of breath respectively. The fifth discipline, *pratyāhāra*, discusses restraint of one's sense organs, while the last three disciplines, *dhāraṇā*, *dhyāna* and *samādhi*, describe the various stages of meditation.

Patañjali lists these eight disciplines in *sūtra* 2.29. They are:

1) *Yama*, Restraint

Yama means restraint with respect to one's actions. This is practised with respect to the following:

a) *Ahiṃsā*, Noninjury

It is to be practised as a discipline wherein one avoids hurting another by thought, word and deed.*

b) *Satya*, Truthfulness

The practice of *Satya* implies consistency between one's thoughts and speech. While speaking the truth, one avoids hurting another by one's words.**

c) *Asteya*, Non-stealing

In practising non-stealing, one does not take things that belong to someone else nor does one desire someone else's belongings.

d) *Brahmacarya*, Celibacy

This discipline is practised by restraining one's senses from the pursuit of sensual pleasures.

e) *Aparigraha*, Absence of Greed

It is difficult to reach a point of total satisfaction through the fulfillment of desires. No matter how much one acquires, one often wants more. This dissatisfaction leads to a sense of inadequacy within oneself which expresses itself in the form of greed. Being alert to and overcoming the tendency requires constant effort and understanding.

2) *Niyama*, Observances

Niyama refers to rules of positive conduct. These rules are self-imposed and practised as a discipline to facilitate one's growth. *Patañjali* describes them as follows:

a) *Śauca*, Purity

Purity is observed with respect to one's environment, body and mind. This observance also includes the consumption of pure foods and avoidance of items such as alcohol and putrid food.

b) *Santoṣa*, Contentment

Santoṣa implies an absence of desire for possessions in excess of one's immediate necessities. One makes a deliberate attempt to simplify one's life and be satisfied with the minimum requirements.

c) *Tapas*, Austerities

Practising austerities as a discipline gives one the capacity to bear discomforts that are inevitable in life. One learns to tolerate the opposites, such as heat and cold and pleasure and pain; and discomforts, such as hunger and thirst. Two types of *mauna*, silence, are included among the austerities mentioned in *aṣṭāṅga-yoga*. The first type of *mauna* is called *kāṣṭha-mauna*, which is refraining from speech and all other forms of expression. The second type of *mauna* is called *ākāra-mauna*, which is refraining from speech and instead using other forms of expression, such as writing and sign language.

d) *Svādhyāya*, Study

The *yoga-śāstra* describes *svādhyāya* as study of the scriptures which lead one to *mokṣa*, liberation. Without study and understanding, all practices and disciplines become mechanical. *Svādhyāya* also includes the repetition of the *mantra*, *om*.

e) *Īśvara-praṇidhāna*, Devotion to the Lord

Īśvara-praṇidhāna is dedicating all actions to *Īśvara*. One appreciates *Īśvara* as the very laws that operate in the creation, and as the giver of the results of all actions. Such an attitude, called *karma-yoga*, helps one develop a mature mind, which is a prerequisite for gaining self-knowledge.

In practising the disciplines of *yama* and *niyama*, one may encounter various obstacles. The *yoga-śāstra* describes a method, called *Pratipakṣa-bhāvanā*, to help one deal with these. *Pratipakṣa-bhāvanā* means deliberately entertaining the opposite thought. If one dislikes another person, one should deliberately think of what is likeable about that person. By seeing the likeable qualities in a person one can neutralise one's dislike towards that person.

3) *Āsana*, Sitting Posture

Āsana is described by *Patañjali* as "*Sthirasukham āsanam*" - a sitting position that is steady and comfortable. In his commentary on the *Yoga-sūtras*,*** *Vyāsa* describes eleven different postures: *padmāsana*, *vīrāsana*, *bhadrāsana*, *svastikāsana*, *daṇḍāsana*, *sopāśraya*, *paryaṅka*, *krauñcaniṣadana*, *hastiniṣadana*, *uṣṭraniṣadana* and *samasamsthāna* (*śavāsana*).

These *āsanas* are meant to relax the body. As the body becomes relaxed, motionless and comfortable, one's mind is available for meditation without any distractions caused by physical discomfort.

4) *Prāṇāyāma*, Breath Control

Prāṇāyāma is defined as the regulation of the movement of air while breathing. This technique requires the temporary suspension of breathing following inhalation and exhalation. The methods of practising *prāṇāyāma* are explained in detail in the *yoga-śāstra*.

The process of breathing is closely associated with the functioning of the mind. When one's mind is agitated, restless and anxious, one's breathing tends to be rapid and shallow. When one's mind is calm and relaxed, one's breathing tends to be deep and slow. By controlling the breathing process with *prāṇāyāma* one can make one's mind calm and ready for meditation.

5) *Pratyāhāra*, Restraint of the Sense Organs

Just as one's mental activity subsides by a process of *prāṇāyāma*, one's sense activities can also be made to subside by the restraint of the sense organs through a discipline called *pratyāhāra*. When the sense organs dissociate from the sense objects, the mind that is associated with them becomes quiet and free from externally directed activity.

6) *Dhāraṇā*

Dhāraṇā consists of fixing one's mind on imaginary points within one's body, called *cakras*, or on external objects, such as sounds or forms. This discipline helps one gain a single-pointedness of the mind, leading to the next step of *dhyāna*.

7) *Dhyāna*

In *dhyāna* the flow of thoughts continues to rest upon the object of *dhāraṇā* without any interruption. The process of *dhyāna* is likened to a continuous flow of oil or honey.

8) *Sāmādhi*

In *aṣṭāṅga-yoga*, *samādhi* is described as a state of mind in which only the object of meditation is present and the mind is as though devoid of thought.

In practising *aṣṭāṅga-yoga* the goal is *citta-vṛtti-nirodha*, the elimination of all thought modifications in the mind. By constant practice of *yoga-āsanas* and *prāṇāyāma*, one learns to sit with oneself for a length of time. Once this is accomplished, the various stages of meditation help one discover a silent, alert mind. These meditations free the mind of its habitual chattering, anxieties and fears and help one discover one's natural state of being. The practice of *aṣṭāṅga-yoga* thus enables one to develop a highly focused, disciplined and contented mind.

* Refer to "Noninjury", Part 6.

** Refer to "Truthfulness", Part 6.

*** For details of these *āsanas* refer to *Vyāsa's* commentary on *sūtra* 2.46 in *Patañjali's Yoga-sūtras*.

EXERCISE

I. Fill in the blanks with the words given below:

eight-fold meditation	*niyama*	mechanical	
Patañjali	*yama*	world	*Vyāsa*
pratipakṣa-bhāvanā	*prāṇāyāma*	*āsana*	*dharma*

1. *Aṣṭāṅga-yoga* was written by ________________.

2. *Aṣṭāṅga-yoga* refers to the ________________ discipline.

3. To live a content life, one must necessarily be in harmony with oneself and the ________________.

4. *Dhāraṇā* , *dhyāna* and *samādhi* describe the various stages of ________________.

5. ________________ and ________________ describe the healthy disposition of a human being and form the basis of the practice of the *Patañjali's* other remaining six disciplines.

6. By constant practice of the *yoga-āsanas* and ________________, one learns to sit with oneself for a length of time.

7. Without study and understanding all practices and disciplines become ________________.

8. Deliberately entertaining the opposite point of view is called ________________.

II. Define the following components of *Aṣṭāṅga-yoga*:

1. *Yama*

   ____

2. *Niyama*

   ____

3. *Āsana*

   ____

4. *Prāṇāyāma*

   ____

5. *Pratyāhāra*

   ____

6. *Dhāraṇā*

   ____

7. *Dhyāna*

   ____

8. *Samādhi*

   ____

III. Answer these questions:

1. Name some of the ways *yama*, restraint, is practised.

2. Which internal function is closely associated with the mind?

3. What are the two types of *mauna*, silence, in *aṣṭāṅga-yoga*?

4. How does *aṣṭāṅga-yoga* help one to develop a mature and disciplined mind?

15100718R00085

Made in the USA
Middletown, DE
23 October 2014